Cubans in Puerto Rico

Cubans in Puerto Rico

Ethnic Economy and Cultural Identity

José A. Cobas

and

Jorge Duany

University Press of Florida
Gainesville/Tallahassee/Tampa/Boca Raton
Pensacola/Orlando/Miami/Jacksonville

02 01 00 99 98 97 6 5 4 3 2 1

Library of Congress Cataloging-in-Publication Data

Cobas, José A.
[Cubanos en Puerto Rico. English]
Cubans in Puerto Rico: ethnic economy and cultural identity / José A. Cobas and Jorge Duany.
p. cm.
Includes bibliographical references and index.
1. Cubans—Puerto Rico—Economic conditions. 2. Immigrants—Puerto Rico—Economic conditions. 3. Cubans—Puerto Rico—Ethnic identity. 4. Puerto Rico—Ethnic relations. I. Duany, Jorge. II. Title.
F1983.C83C6313 1997
305.868'729107295—dc21 96-39603

The University Press of Florida is the scholarly publishing agency for the State University System of Florida, comprised of Florida A & M University, Florida Atlantic University, Florida International University, Florida State University, University of Central Florida, University of Florida, University of North Florida, University of South Florida, and University of West Florida.

University Press of Florida
15 Northwest 15th Street
Gainesville, FL 32611

Contents

List of Tables

Acknowledgments

I am grateful to many. The first person with whom I discussed Cubans in Puerto Rico was Alejandro Portes, who suggested I look at the middleman minority literature. When I began to plan my study, Edna Bonacich was kind enough to provide me with many materials, including her unpublished book manuscript.

This book utilizes data from a survey that I directed in Puerto Rico which was supported by a grant from the National Science Foundation. I would like to thank Agustín Ayuso for his help during the very early stages of the survey. Miguel Valencia was responsible for the technical aspects of the sample selection. His ample experience and generous spirit made life much easier for me. I would like to express my appreciation to Walter Zenner and Silvia Pedraza for their most helpful comments on the manuscript. None of them bears any responsibility for any shortcomings the book may have.

I would also like to thank my wife, Brenda, for helping in so many ways, and for the wonderful gift of Andrew, our son.

José A. Cobas
Tempe, Arizona

Several persons and institutions helped me with this book. First, Michel S. Laguerre and Stanley Brandes ably supervised my dissertation at the University of California, Berkeley. Through Berkeley's Center for Latin American Studies I received two grants from the Tinker Foundation to travel to Puerto Rico. Marian Z. Sugano offered a sustained intellectual challenge during those years. During my stay at the University of Florida's Center for Latin American Studies, I benefited from the interest that my colleagues

Helen I. Safa, Glaucio Soares, and Emilio Bejel showed in my work on Cuban migration. Carlos Santiago, from the University at Albany (SUNY), was kind to provide us with unpublished census data on Puerto Rico.

In Puerto Rico, Himilce Esteve stimulated my interest in Cuban migration and offered insightful comments on the manuscript. Julio Sánchez, my former high school teacher, helped me clarify several characteristics of Puerto Rico's Cuban community. The Academic Computing Service at the Universidad del Sagrado Corazón aided me with the gathering and analysis of survey data. My thanks go to Sandra Santos and Ricardo Barahona.

The Academic Research Center at the Universidad del Sagrado Corazón provided me release time from teaching during 1991–92, which allowed me to work on the manuscript. I would like to acknowledge the support of the center's former director, my friend and colleague César A. Rey. My former secretary, Angie Rivera, amply deserves my thanks for her three years of collaboration. To the university's former president José Alberto Morales I extend my gratitude for his support of academic research, of which this book is an example.

Several friends and relatives were kind enough to read the manuscript: María del Carmen Baerga; María Pi; Helen I. Safa; my brother Luis Duany; my mother, Mirtha Blanco; and my father, Rafael Duany. I have also been fortunate to enjoy the unconditional support of my wife, Diana Johnson, in all of my academic pursuits. My daughter, Patricia, has respected her father's intellectual work, even though she does not understand it yet. This book is dedicated to the loving memory of my mother and to the future of my son, Jorge Andrés.

Jorge Duany
Rio Piedras, Puerto Rico

Introduction

The year 1959 was of singular importance in Cuban history. A group of revolutionaries led by Fidel Castro overthrew Fulgencio Batista, a hated tyrant. Their triumph was celebrated with unusual enthusiasm not only in Cuba but abroad as well. The bearded youths who descended from the mountains captured the romantic spirit of many.

But in trying to revamp Cuban society, the revolution caused dissidence. Although the discontent initially centered in the propertied classes, people of more moderate means, including many who fought in the ranks of the revolution, became alienated by the unexpected extremism of the revolution. Some of the discontent opted for armed opposition. A much larger group chose exile, mainly in the United States, about ninety miles away and a sympathetic and generous host to the émigrés. The bulk of the exiles settled in the continental United States, principally in Miami and to a lesser extent in New York and New Jersey. A smaller wave went to Puerto Rico, mainly to the San Juan area.

The migration of Cuban refugees to Puerto Rico occurred for a variety of reasons. In 1960 and 1961 an initial wave consisting mostly of technicians and professionals was invited by then governor Luis Muñoz Marín (Volsky 1974). These and subsequent migrants were attracted by several features of the island: first, Spanish is the vernacular in Puerto Rico; second, culture, climate, and terrain resemble those of Cuba; third, Puerto Rico's economic growth created economic opportunities in the 1960s; and fourth, Puerto Rico has close political ties with the United States. This last element was of utmost importance to a group of individuals who, having been traumatized by their experiences in Cuba, believed that another Marxist revolution could not occur in an island so closely associated with the United States. As a relatively large Cuban community grew in San Juan, kinship and friendship ties among the exiles fueled more migration to Puerto Rico.

The Cuban community in Puerto Rico exhibits an interesting combination of economic and social characteristics. As will be documented later, a substantial percentage of these people are in business for themselves or work for a coethnic. Many show a propensity to maintain friendship and kinship ties within the in-group. They are regarded by some members of the host society with a mixture of admiration, suspicion, and resentment. Given this combination of traits, some observers have called Cubans in Puerto Rico the "Jews of the Caribbean." This is an insightful sobriquet, for Jews are one of the classic examples of a middleman group. In this book we will argue that Cubans in Puerto Rico constitute such a group.

Middleman groups may be defined as culturally distinct communities that specialize in the distribution of goods and services within the host economy. Middleman groups do not occupy the lowest socio-economic positions but rather concentrate in the middle and upper strata. They are prone to concentrate in trade, finance, and other intermediary positions from which they serve an out-group clientele. They tend to retain their cultural identity. Finally, they often experience antagonism from members of the receiving society.

Armstrong (1976) uses the term "mobilized diasporas" to refer to groups that enjoy material and cultural advantages when compared to other members of the society. Mobilized diasporas frequently adapt to the receiving society by playing the role of middleman group. However, groups such as Cubans in Miami have adapted not as a middleman group but through an "ethnic enclave," that is, a concentration of interrelated businesses that occupy a distinct territory and serve primarily the in-group (Light et al. 1994; Portes and Bach 1985). Later we will discuss the differences between middleman groups and ethnic enclaves. We will show that the socio-economic characteristics of Cubans in Puerto Rico differ from those of their counterparts in the United States.

The study of middleman groups requires examination of diverse social phenomena. In studying them it is necessary to address, among other things, the association between class and ethnic identity, the question of why some middleman groups persist while others are transitory, the relationship between the middleman group and diverse classes in the host society, and why some middleman groups become minorities.[1] These questions are typically found in studies of middleman groups. In addition, cultural similarities between Cubans and Puerto Ricans allow us to deal with another important question that has been overlooked, namely, how the adaptation of a middleman group differs from the typical pattern of those whose cultural differences with the host society are minimal.

The thesis of this book consists essentially of three interrelated propositions. First, Cubans in Puerto Rico share many of the characteristics of middleman groups. Second, these characteristics help explain the reception of the Cuban community by the host society. Third, Cubans will not become a permanent middleman group but will eventually join the middle and upper strata of Puerto Rican society.

The study of Cubans in Puerto Rico is important for various reasons. First, social scientists have tended to ignore foreign migration into Puerto Rico, concentrating instead on Puerto Rican migration to the United States. Despite massive out-migration since the 1940s, foreign in-migration, particularly from Cuba and the Dominican Republic, has increased in Puerto Rico since the 1960s. This book attempts to balance the image of Puerto Rico as not only a source of migrants to the United States but also as a receiver of outsiders. Second, the study of Cubans in Puerto Rico as a middleman group permits novel analyses. Up to now the middleman group model has been used predominantly to analyze the economic adaptation of ethnic groups that are culturally dissimilar from the receiving society. It is necessary to test the predictions of the model with a group such as Cubans in Puerto Rico, who differ little culturally from the receiving society.

Finally, the reception and adaptation of Cubans in Puerto Rico have been largely overlooked until now. Most of the available literature on Cuban immigrants has emphasized the socio-economic adaptation of Cubans in Miami. The circumstances surrounding the Cuban diaspora in Puerto Rico differ significantly from the better-known situation of the exiles in the mainland. The Puerto Rican setting provides an opportunity to understand the changing nature of intergroup relations and immigrant group adaptation in different geographic and cultural contexts. In brief, the study of Cubans in Puerto Rico will shed new light on the Cuban exile experience.

A Methodological Note

To address the preceding issues, this book combines two studies carried out independently by the authors. Cobas, a sociologist, directed a survey in 1981–82 that yielded statistical data on the Cuban community of San Juan.

Duany, an anthropologist, conducted fieldwork among Cuban exiles in San Juan in 1983 and 1984. The authors updated their results in the early 1990s with additional personal interviews, participant observation, and census data. These studies emanated not just out of intellectual curiosity but also from the authors' experiences as Cuban immigrants residing in the United States and Puerto Rico. As a result, the book reflects professional analyses as well as personal experiences.

Cobas's survey comprised two stages. During the first stage, the questionnaire was constructed and pretested. These preliminary interviews revealed ambiguities and omissions in the questionnaire, which were corrected in the final version. The second stage comprised the selection of the sample.[2] A total of twenty-eight sampling clusters from the San Juan Standard Metropolitan Statistical Area were selected with probability proportional to size. The sampling clusters comprised a) areas listed in the 1970 census, b) new housing developments, and c) condominiums.

The areas listed in the 1970 census were: Caparra Terrace, Country Club, Milaville, Minillas, Miramar, Vedado, Venus Gardens, Villa Nevares, El Cerezal, Ocean Park, and Park Gardens in San Juan. From Bayamón the following were chosen: Santa Rosa, Villa Contessa, and Sierra Bayamón. From Carolina the following were selected: Jardines de Country Club, Valle Arriba Heights, and Villamar. Finally, from Guaynabo were chosen: Ponce de León, Torrimar, Golden Gates, and Tintillo Gardens. The new housing developments were Colinas de Monte Carlo in San Juan; Villa España and Río Hondo in Bayamón; and Levittown Lakes in Toa Baja. The condominiums were Sky Towers in San Juan, Garden Hills in Guaynabo, and Laguna Gardens in Carolina.

Cuban college students (six women and one man) were employed to conduct the interviews. In our judgment, their age range and nationality made them less threatening to the subjects, an important consideration in light of the sensitive nature of some of the questions. Each interviewer was directed to a randomly selected housing unit in each cluster and instructed to visit every third dwelling after that. Fully employed adult males were identified and, if possible, interviewed on the spot. (The reason for the all-male sample was that there were insufficient resources to obtain samples of males and females.) Whether or not Cubans resided in the selected unit, the interviewer solicited information about Cubans living in the vicinity and compiled a secondary list. A limit of thirty interviews per cluster was set, and if at the end of the systematic canvasing the interviewers had not reached the limit, respondents were added from the secondary list. The selection procedure yielded a total of 261 eligible individuals, 220 of whom were interviewed. This represents a response rate of 84%, which was satisfactory for our purposes.

Duany carried out the initial fieldwork for his project between July 1983 and December 1984. His goal was to document Cuban activities in various settings in San Juan. To discover the principles that guided the exiles' social relations, he used participant observation extensively. Because he was born in Cuba and raised in Puerto Rico, Duany had many connections with the group before entering the field. Among them were the two major Cuban institutions in San Juan: the Círculo Cubano de Puerto Rico and the Unión de Cubanos en el Exilio. Duany attended their activities, read their literature, and interviewed their members and leaders. But the principal contacts were established informally through friends, relatives, and acquaintances.

The project was originally based on relatively open and unstructured interviews, but it soon became clear that this strategy was impractical because it would be difficult to compare the subjects' responses. Hence, a standardized questionnaire was constructed and, after being pretested, administered to a representative sample of Cubans in San Juan. Although the sample was not selected at random but rather was chosen proportionately with respect to age and occupation, these data will be used in the book to complement Cobas's survey.

To triangulate the data from the interviews, a content analysis was done of a sample of exile publications in Puerto Rico. Extensive thematic data were extracted from magazines such as *Casa de Cuba* and *Vida de Club*, periodicals such as *La Crónica* and *Cuba Independiente y Democrática*, and several yearbooks. In addition, a demographic study was completed on the basis of Cuban marriage licenses in San Juan between 1970 and 1983. The sample for this study included 2,034 Cuban marriage partners for four years chosen at random: 1970, 1973, 1980, and 1983. In sum, this book uses extensive and diverse sources of information on Cuban migration to Puerto Rico.

Organization and Contents of the Book

Chapter 1 discusses the middleman group model. The review of the literature reveals a controversy regarding the application of the classic model—an ideal type developed in light of the experiences of permanent middleman groups such as Jews and Armenians—to the situation of contemporary middleman groups. This chapter discusses the main criticisms against the classic model and proposes revisions to make it more relevant to contemporary cases. An updated model, chapter 1 argues, helps explain the socio-economic characteristics of many groups concentrated in ethnic economies, such as Cubans in Puerto Rico.

Chapter 2 discusses the background of the Cuban exodus. Popular reaction has ranged from the positive image of this exodus as a "Golden Exile" to the negative characterization of Cuban immigrants as "dirty worms." Academic studies question both extremes and propose a more complex analysis of the migration of almost one million individuals from Cuba to the United States.

Chapter 3 describes the Cuban community of Puerto Rico. The social, economic, and political characteristics of this community differ from those of other Cuban exile settlements. Among other dissimilarities, Cubans in Puerto Rico show a higher degree of occupational specialization than their counterparts in the United States. While Cubans in Puerto Rico tend to concentrate in sales and managerial occupations, in the United States Cubans are more dispersed throughout the occupational structure.

Chapter 4 applies the revised model of middleman groups to Cubans in Puerto Rico. The socio-economic profile of Cubans in Puerto Rico fits the middleman model, particularly in terms of income, education, and occupation. Additionally, few Cubans are employed in Puerto Rican businesses but rather tend to work for themselves, a coethnic, or another foreigner. This form of occupational specialization has important consequences for the cultural identity of Cubans. However, Cubans differ from other middleman groups in that they are not highly clannish. Cultural, linguistic, and religious similarities with the receiving society have contributed to the integration of Cuban exiles with their hosts. Such integration, however, has been largely limited to the Puerto Rican middle and upper strata, and the strong cultural similarities have not averted the development of antagonistic relations between the two groups.

Chapter 5 examines the association between the social characteristics of Cuban exiles and their mode of economic adaptation. In particular, Cuban exiles who participate in the ethnic economy show higher attachment to the in-group than those who work in the general economy. Moreover, employees of Cuban businesses are more estranged from the receiving society than others. The evidence thus suggests that class differences manifest themselves even within the ethnic economy.

Chapters 6, 7, and 8 represent, respectively, case studies of Casa Cuba, other Cuban voluntary associations, and the Cuban press in Puerto Rico. Casa Cuba is the oldest and largest Cuban institution in Puerto Rico and shows the historical evolution of the Cuban community from the 1940s to the 1990s. In the beginning the club consisted of a small and tightly knit group of Cuban immigrants in Puerto Rico. Subsequently the club's character changed to reflect the interests of exiles who left after the Cuban revolution and who became a middleman group. The existence of Casa Cuba, Unión de Cubanos en el Exilio, and other Cuban associations described in chapter 7 shows the persistence of Cubans' cultural identity and demonstrates their efforts to promote a positive image for the group. The Cuban exile press, analyzed in chapter 8, has also fulfilled an important function. Above all, the Cuban press has supported the social solidarity of the exiles and promoted their economic specialization.

Finally, the conclusion summarizes our results and discusses the implications of the study beyond the situation of Cuban exiles. Our findings, interpreted in light of an updated middleman model, suggest that the model is still useful to examine the impact of ethnic economy specialization on immigrants' cultural identity.

Although the Cuban community of Puerto Rico is this book's main concern, the analysis has wider relevance. Our perspective is based on the middleman group model, and our conclusions may shed light on the experiences of similar groups in other social contexts. Consequently, we hope to contribute to sociological and anthropological theories on middleman groups. At the same time, we intend to show that the experiences of Cubans in Puerto Rico are better understood in a comparative perspective that draws from the histories of other groups who share similar socio-economic experiences.

1

Middleman Groups

An Overview

Immigrant and ethnic groups use different adaptation strategies according to their own resources and inclinations as well as the conditions of the local society. Some groups tend to concentrate as workers in the peripheral sectors of the general economy, while others show a substantial agglomeration in an ethnic economy. Such an economy includes business owners and their employees, who tend to be coethnics (Bonacich and Modell 1980; Light et al. 1994). One of the modes of adaptation followed by groups that concentrate in ethnic economies is to play the role of middleman group. In this book the adaptation of Cubans in Puerto Rico as a middleman group will be discussed.

Origins of the Study of Middleman Groups

The systematic study of middleman groups began with analyses of Jewish diasporas conducted by Marx, Weber, and Simmel. Marx (1964) pointed out the connection between the concentration of European Jews in commercial occupations and their ethnic identity. His solution to the "Jewish Question," that is, the lack of integration of Jews to European society, was for Jews to abandon their traditional economic pursuits. Economic assimilation, in other words, would produce social integration.

Weber (1958) was interested in the role played by different groups in the development of rational capitalism in Western Europe. He concluded that adherents of Calvinism and other Protestant sects possessed a worldly asceticism that was highly consonant with modern capitalism. In another context, Weber (1978a, 614) raised a related issue: Why did Jews not develop a significant industrial bourgeoisie? Weber asserted that, among other reasons, the study of Jewish law was more compatible with economic pursuits such as money lending and trade than with manufacture.

Simmel explained the tendency among Jews to specialize in trade as a result of their stranger status. As he put it:

> Throughout the history of economics the stranger everywhere appears as the trader, or the trader as stranger. . . . Trade can always absorb more people than primary production; it is, therefore, the sphere indicated for the stranger, who intrudes as a supernumerary, so to speak, into a group in which the economic positions are actually occupied—the classic example is the history of European Jews. (1964, 403)

The pioneering efforts of these classic scholars, particularly Weber and Simmel, stimulated the work of later sociologists, such as Stonequist (1937), Park (1950a, 1950b), and Becker (1956). They observed that other ethnic groups shared the tendency of Jewish diasporas to specialize in trade and kindred occupations. The contributions of these later sociologists, together with the writings of contemporary scholars, resulted in the "classic" middleman group model.

The Classic Middleman Group Model

The classic middleman model represents an ideal type. The discussion that follows shows middleman groups settling in certain types of societies, evoking a predictable response from the receiving population, and showing a cluster of socioeconomic characteristics. It also posits interconnections among these traits.

According to the classic model, middleman groups are found in nonindustrialized societies (Light and Bonacich 1988, 17–18). Their principal distinguishing characteristic is that they concentrate in businesses that serve the out-group. They do not invest in cumbersome lines such as manufacture but rather prefer portable endeavors such as retail trade, finance, labor contracting, rent collection, money lending, brokering, and independent professions, such as law and medicine (Bonacich 1973). This propensity to concentrate in certain forms of economic activity is rooted in their experiences as sojourning peoples, which make middleman groups loath to take up businesses that are difficult to move or liquidate. Small businesses are ideal economic pursuits for middleman groups because they can be sold or otherwise disposed of with relative ease when group members need to move.

Middleman groups dominate one or more business lines (Bonacich 1973) because, as group members enter a type of business, they use their contacts and knowledge to help coethnics enter the same line. Members of middleman groups who do not work for themselves work for coethnics or foreigners. They rarely work for locals.

Middleman group businesses have been called "precapitalist" because relations among owners and between owners and employees are based on noneconomic criteria such as trust and loyalty. Owners typically help each other through loans and business tips (Light 1972). Additionally, "if wage labor is needed, members of the extended family or of regional associations are preferred. . . . Employees work excessively long hours for low or no wages and are loyal to the owner"; in return for their loyalty, employees "are likely to become partners or to receive training and aid in setting up their own businesses in the same line" (Bonacich 1973, 586).

Middleman groups' businesses are spread throughout the community to serve an out-group clientele. Middleman groups serve out-group clients for two reasons: first, the number of coethnics is insufficient to support middleman businesses (Light 1972); and second, middleman businesses fill the "status gap," that is, they perform needed economic services that members of the upper class of the dominant group do not want to exploit and occupants of the lower classes are unable to pursue (Bonacich and Modell 1980). Trade and money lending are examples of economic opportunities that the dominant group's upper class does not pursue because such activities would reduce its prestige and that the lower classes cannot aspire to because they lack the resources. Accordingly, middleman groups "serve as economic liaison between those who might service . . . the lower strata but choose not to, and the lower strata who cannot perform these services for themselves" (Rinder 1958, 254). Local elites often support middleman groups because they perform the useful function of serving the receiving society's lower classes.

Middleman groups are not indigenous but rather originate in migration (Purcell 1948). Middleman groups have a higher level of learning, greater ability with foreign languages, and more extensive international networks than members of the receiving society. These qualifications render them adept at foreign trade, a skill that makes them valuable to local elites. Consequently, local elites confer special privileges on middleman groups (Armstrong 1976; Blalock 1967), such as exemption from military service. But local elites also impose restrictions on middleman groups in other spheres. In response to political pressure from other members of the host society, elites may deny middleman group members the right to own land or occupy certain professions as well as eligibility for the armed services' officer corps.

Middleman groups experience antagonism, frequently face efforts to expel them from the host society, and occasionally are victims of genocide. Being set apart by a different culture and customs, they arouse prejudice and discrimination. Their economic success makes them targets of envy and resentment. When host society hostility toward the middleman group becomes severe, elites may withdraw their support for political reasons. Additionally, local elites may use middleman groups as scapegoats, blaming them for social ills for which the group is not even remotely responsible, thus diverting public discontent away from the dominant class. The discrimination and antagonism experienced by middleman groups render them minorities, which explains why many scholars refer to them as "middleman minorities."

Middleman groups are not the only ethnic groups that arouse antagonism from host societies. What distinguishes middleman groups from others is that, because of their economic situation, they are in a better position to parry attacks from the outside. Such an ability, however, sometimes works against middleman groups, because their capacity to defend themselves makes them more difficult to control, and this, in turn, provokes drastic measures (Bonacich 1973).

Middleman groups have the reputation of being clannish. As discussed earlier, middleman business owners help each other and prefer to hire coethnics. A long history of persecution makes middleman group members wary of others and fosters in them a stranger mentality. Religious beliefs, traditions, or laws forbid marriage with out-group members. Middleman groups retain their own culture and as a result stand out from others because of their customs, diet, religion, language, or mode of dress.

In her highly influential article, Bonacich (1973) hypothesizes connections among the middleman minority's major traits. The figure on the nex page shows a diagram of these connections. The diagram identifies four major variables in the study of middleman groups: (1) sojourning and stranger orientation; (2) in-group solidarity; (3) ethnic economy specialization; and (4) host society antagonism. A sojourning outlook and a stranger orientation increase the propensity to concentrate in a small business ethnic economy rather than in the general economy. Sojourning and the stranger orientation also have a positive effect on in-group solidarity, as sojourners and strangers tend to establish relationships with other coethnics rather than with members of the wider society, with whom they have less affinity. In-group solidarity facilitates movement into business, as prospective entrepreneurs tap coethnics for resources such as loans, labor, and business tips. Movement into business, in turn, influences solidarity, as business owners maintain access to resources by sustaining their good standing among coethnics. Movement into business arouses antagonism on the part of customers and business rivals. Hostility also arises from the group's solidarity which provokes charges of clannishness. Faced with antagonism, the group closes ranks and becomes more solidary and more reluctant to set roots in

Interconnections among middleman group traits.

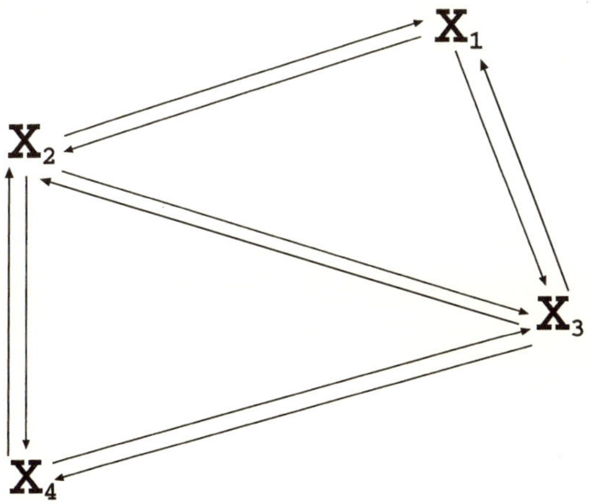

X_1 = Sojourning and stranger orientation
X_2 = In-group solidarity
X_3 = Ethnic economy specialization
X_4 = Host society antagonism

the receiving society. Finally, hostility closes opportunities in the wider economy, which forces ethnic group members to seek opportunities in the ethnic economy.[1]

In sum, classic middleman groups are sojourning peoples who because of their language skills and international connections are particularly adept at commerce. They settle in nonindustrialized societies where they are allowed to do business because trade is disdained by the upper class. They are clannish peoples who at once receive privileges from the elite and are denied rights available to the general populace. They are frequent targets of societal antagonism and often are used as scapegoats by the elite.

Reexamination of the Classic Model

Seeing the classic middleman model as accurate is appealing for several reasons. First, as Zenner states, it "combines an interest in ethnicity—generally seen as a primordial factor—with a search for socioeconomic explanations of social phenomena" (1991, xiii). Second, it draws from the fascinating historical experiences of groups such as Jews and Armenians, who served as traders for generations, longed for a return to their homeland, struggled to maintain their ethnic identity, and faced persecution repeatedly.[2] But in spite of its appeal, the classic middleman model has been the subject of several criticisms.

Some authors (Aldrich and Waldinger 1990) assert that the classic middleman model is ahistorical because its components do not reflect the actual history of middleman groups but instead describe characteristics that may have applied at particular points in time and in only some social settings. It is not difficult to find instances in which middleman groups departed from the classic model. For example, the overseas Chinese intermarried with members of the host society and showed a considerable degree of assimilation over the years (Landon 1941; Skinner 1957). So have Jews in diverse settings (Zenner 1991). Aldrich and Waldinger (1990) further question the characterization of middleman groups as precapitalist in orientation and retaining archaic practices such as hiring coethnics.

In their study of Koreans in Los Angeles, Light and Bonacich (1988) found the classic middleman model to be too restrictive. In their view, the model is narrow in three respects: first, it is oriented to underdeveloped economies of the third world; second, it assumes that the wider society disdains trade; and third, it stresses wandering groups whose mode of economic adaptation arose as a historic response to ethnic discrimination.

Portes and Manning (1986) do not find flaws with the model as such but are critical of the way in which it has been used. They assert that the middleman model has been incorrectly applied to groups whose experiences are better described by another model, the ethnic enclave. According to Portes and Manning, Cubans in Miami and Jews in Manhattan adapted as ethnic enclaves, not middleman groups.

To be sure, as Portes and Manning (1986) explain, the middleman group and ethnic enclave models have points of convergence. Both emphasize that ethnic entrepreneurs rely on the in-group for business resources and cheap labor, and both stress that employment in ethnic businesses provides opportunities for moving into self-employment. But the two models differ in important ways. Middleman groups comprise small immigrant populations that specialize in commercial roles. Their businesses are dispersed throughout the community. The middleman group is accepted by elites but resented by the masses. Ethnic enclaves, on the other hand, are characteristic of large immigrant populations whose businesses are spatially concentrated. Enclave firms are not mainly concentrated in commercial lines but also include agriculture, light manufacturing, and construction enterprises. Lastly, ethnic enclaves arouse hostility both from elites and masses.[3] Therefore, the two models are not inter-changeable, and care should be taken to apply them properly.

Horowitz (1985) is critical of the emphasis on class-based conflict found in the classic model, particularly in Bonacich's (1973) synthesis. As stated earlier, the model expects business rivalries and conflict with customers to provoke antagonism against middleman groups. According to Horowitz (1985, 108, 113), the ethnic division of labor in many societies limits the competition among ethnic groups over the same occupations and business lines. Accordingly, the classic model exaggerates the degree of economically based ethnic conflict. Additionally, Horowitz (1985, 123–24) questions the assumption that conflict of interest between middleman group traders and their clients is inevitable. It is doubtful that customers always perceive traders as exploiters and are not aware of the services that traders provide.

In spite of the preceding criticisms, these authors do not propose a total rejection of the middleman model. Aldrich and Waldinger (1990, 121) believe that the classic model has descriptive value in contemporary societies. Several contemporary ethnic groups, such as Koreans in the United States, Indians in Great Britain, and Moroccans in France, concentrate in businesses that depend mainly on transactions with out-group members. Consequently, Aldrich and Waldinger (1990) propose the term "pseudomiddleman minority" to distinguish contemporary ethnic groups that specialize in trade from classic middleman groups. Finally, Light and Bonacich (1988, 17) see value in the middleman model for three reasons: first, it addresses the issue of ethnic group overrepresentation in business; second, it emphasizes the capacity of some groups to establish businesses in adverse economic contexts; and third, it explains the tensions that arise when an alien group serves as a buffer between the elite and the masses.

In sum, critics assert that the classic middleman group model is not applicable to all contemporary ethnic groups that specialize in an ethnic economy. Other authors find the model ahistorical because it assumes that minorities that concentrate in trade fill disdained commercial positions, are permanent wandering peoples possessed of a sojourning orientation, receive special favors from the elites, and run precapitalist enterprises. Still others take issue with the model's emphasis on class-based conflict. These objections notwithstanding, these scholars still find value in the middleman model.

An Evaluation of Middleman Group Theory

Many of the difficulties associated with the middleman model can be attributed to the fact that it represents an ideal type. The ideal type is an analytic tool developed by Weber (1978b, 1:18–22), who used it extensively. One of the best-known applications of this research strategy is Weber's analysis of the relationship between the Puritan ethos and the growth of modern capitalism (Weber 1958). Once an ideal type has been abstracted from historical data, then empirical instances of the phenomenon in question are compared with the abstract model and departures are analyzed. That is why many of the previously discussed criticisms against the classic middleman model are puzzling. First, the critics object that the model does not apply in many settings and historical times. But ideal types were devised precisely to analyze such departures. Second, they offer alternative abstract types, such as the "pseudomiddleman" model, as a solution to the difficulties accompanying the middleman model. But such alternative models can be faulted for sharing some of the same deficiencies that the middleman model is purported to have.

We find that the classic middleman model identifies key variables in the study of middleman groups: duration of the middleman status, minority status of the middleman group, use of precapitalist business practices, and relations between middleman groups and elites. In the discussion that follows we address factors that affect these variables.

Duration of Middleman Status

Contemporary analyses recognize that the duration of the middleman status for a group depends on factors such as the existence of a homeland to which one day the group may return (Armstrong 1976), the availability of opportunities in the majority-dominated economy, and the ability of the group to take advantage of these opportunities (Bonacich and Modell 1980). While some groups, such as Jews in medieval Europe, persist for generations in the middleman role, others, such as the Japanese in the United States, fulfill this role for a briefer period.

Minority Status

Among the characteristics that affect the probability that middleman groups will face prejudice and discrimination in the host society are the receiving society's tolerance, religious and cultural differences separating the middleman group from the receiving society, and the existence of nationalist movements (Stryker 1958; Zenner 1991). Although Jews and Armenians faced prejudice in different settings for long periods of time, other groups who have played the middleman role, such as the Parsis in India (Stryker 1958) and Quakers and Scots in the United States and Canada, did not (Zenner 1991).

Antimiddleman prejudice can grow into open conflict. Sometimes the source of the conflict is friction between middleman traders and their customers. But conflict may have a noneconomic basis. Bonacich, for example, attributes part of the antagonism against middleman groups to accusations of "disloyalty to the countries in which they reside" (1973, 591). Charges of disloyalty, she adds, are aggravated in postcolonial societies by "the fact that middleman minorities tend to be allied with the colonial masters" (1973, 591).

The threat of minority status explains why middleman groups strive to improve their public image. When negative stereotypes about them emerge, middleman groups do not accept them passively. Middleman groups realize that a great deal of the antagonism directed at them is the result of their negative image as clannish and greedy traders. Aware of this public perception, middleman groups strive to project a different image (Zenner 1991). Such efforts help explain demonstrations of patriotism on the part of Susi Berbers of Casablanca as well as American Jews' charitable contributions and attempts to minimize cultural differences with the receiving society. An important part of the behavior of middleman groups reflects their efforts at improving their image.

Prejudice and discrimination affect whether or not the middleman group assimilates into the host society, but the association is not perfect. Some middleman groups, such as Germans in Imperial Russia, faced little or no prejudice and established social and marital bonds with the upper classes of the host society. The Portuguese in Brazil offer an interesting example of a middleman group that, while being vilified by some members of the receiving society, was integrating with others (Hahner 1976).

The propensity of group members to assimilate depends not only on the receiving society but also on their own inclinations. Members who participate in the ethnic economy retain a higher attachment to the in-group and are less likely to assimilate than others (Bonacich and Modell 1980).

Precapitalist Business Practices

The degree to which ethnic businesses rely on coethnics for resources such as labor is contingent on factors such as the availability of in-group workers. When in-group labor is not abundant or cheap, out-group members are hired. In-group labor is not particularly plentiful or cheap when unemployment is high and work opportunities are meager in the receiving society. Such settings are not attractive to the working class, and the ranks of immigrants will include few workers and many entrepreneurs. However, ethnic businesses may still employ some coethnics, particularly in positions of trust.

Relations Between Middleman Groups and Elites

This issue comprises three questions. First, do middleman groups play an economically useful role in contemporary societies? Second, do elites favor middleman groups? Third, are elite attitudes related to the economic role played by middleman groups?

Middleman groups were valuable in the past because they performed important services for the elite (Armstrong 1976). Middleman groups were appreciated not only because they filled the status gap but also because they had the best skills and connections required for international trade. In today's world, commercial skills and connections are found in many sectors of society. However, middleman groups remain particularly useful in one area of economic activity: they often own liquor stores, gas stations, and convenience stores in blighted urban areas (Bonacich 1987). It would be inaccurate to equate operating a business in the ghetto with filling the status gap or conducting international trade. Nonetheless, ethnic traders perform a service for the wider society by selling their products in areas that many members of the dominant group prefer to avoid.

Concerning the second question, whether middleman minorities receive support from the elite, critics answer no. For example, Aldrich and Waldinger assert: "Elite support of middleman minorities is a characteristic of traditional, state-building, and colonial situations" (1990, 120). In other words, elite support of middleman groups is a thing of the past. But this is only partly true. Although middleman groups are not sponsored by the upper classes in the style of past centuries, the modern state has supported "minority business," and contemporary groups have received many state favors (Aldrich and Waldinger 1990, 122; Pedraza-Bailey 1985). Thus, in the United States groups such as Vietnamese and Cuban immigrants have received business loans, incentives for relocations, and other forms of aid.

Regarding the issue of whether elite support is tied to the economic role played by middleman groups, the answer is that political factors play a more important part than economic factors. A salient element in the American state's interest in Cuban and Vietnamese immigrants is that both of these groups were refugees from communism, and their odysseys from their homelands supported the anticommunist ideology of the 1960s and 1970s (Pedraza-Bailey 1985). The apparently less sympathetic treatment by American authorities of South Korean entrepreneurs (Light and Bonacich 1988, ch. 12), who are not refugees from communism, supports this interpretation. Additionally, these economic experiences of refugees from communism have bolstered the legitimacy of the status quo. The refugees' economic success stories are "held up as examples for others to emulate. They demonstrate to everyone that America is still a land of opportunity" (Bonacich 1987, 446).

To sum up, in the past middleman groups performed useful economic functions, and local elites appreciated these services and supported middleman groups. In contemporary societies the economic functions of middleman groups are not as essential as before, and elites are not as supportive of middleman groups as in the past. However, in contemporary societies middleman groups still fulfill economic responsibilities that others prefer to avoid. At least in the United States, the government has supported the development of ethnic businesses as well as programs that help immigrants who concentrate in business. This support seems to be related to the political implications of the escape from communism of some middleman groups. With the modifications pointed out above, the ideas regarding the status breach and relations between elites and middleman groups are still pertinent.

Conclusion

This chapter has reviewed many of the critiques against the classic middleman group model. Researchers have applied this model in settings in which it did not fit. Many of the other criticisms, however, are based on a misunderstanding of the ideal type as a tool of social analysis. It is important to remember that the classic middleman model was inspired to a great extent by the work of Weber, whose study of the economic behavior of Jews was part of a larger concern with the association of religion and the growth of capitalism in the West. In his studies Weber constructed an ideal type of Jewish economic behavior, much of which found its way into the classic middleman group model. Weber used the ideal type to analyze departures from the abstract model, not to provide a description of middleman groups that would apply in most settings.

But although ideal types can be most helpful in some circumstances, they have their limits. For our needs, we do not require a Weberian abstract model of the middleman group but rather a set of propositions that help explain variations in form of economic adaptation, in-group solidarity, and host-society reception experienced by middleman groups. These propositions will help in our analysis of the experiences of Cuban exiles in Puerto Rico. In the next chapter we begin this analysis by providing the historical background of the Cuban exodus to Puerto Rico.

2

Background of the Cuban Exodus

As pointed out in chapter 1, middleman groups usually originate from migration, not from conquest or colonization. This is the reason that some scholars refer to them as "people of the diaspora." But in contrast to immigrants who leave their countries because of economic necessity, middleman groups frequently originate from the privileged strata of their societies of origin (Bonacich 1973; Bonacich and Modell 1980; Waldinger et al. 1990). As noted before, classic middleman groups, such as the overseas Chinese and the Jews, tended to be more literate and educated than the general population of their host societies. Similar characteristics are found in contemporary middleman groups. They include a high proportion of managers, professionals, technical workers, sales representatives, and skilled workers. Such was the case of many Koreans, Vietnamese, Indians, and Cubans who began arriving in the United States in the 1950s.

This chapter will review the circumstances that shaped the massive migration of Cubans to the United States and Puerto Rico.[1] First the prevailing views on Cuban exiles found in the press and academic writings will be identified. Subsequently we will analyze the main stages of the Cuban exodus since 1959, followed later by an examination of the socioeconomic adaptation and acculturation of the immigrants. Finally, the major Cuban communities in the United States will be compared and contrasted.

Golden Exiles or Dirty Worms?

On January 8, 1959, Fidel Castro and his guerrillas arrived in Havana, followed by thousands of euphoric Cubans. The overthrow of the Batista dictatorship (1952–58) unleashed the first successful Marxist-Leninist revolution of the Americas as well as the largest refugee influx into the United States in recent history. Only the Vietnamese have posed a comparable challenge to the U.S. government in the last three decades. The 1990 census counted 1,043,932 Cubans in the United States, principally in Florida and New Jersey (U.S. Department of Commerce 1991, table 1). Other important Cuban settlements are found in New York, California, and Puerto Rico. Currently, Cuban immigrants represent around 10 percent of the Cuban population.

Although much has been written on Cuban exiles in the last three decades, a good portion of this literature is loaded with distorted views. On the one hand, the U.S. press has tended to depict Cuban immigrants as latter-day pursuers of the American dream. Because Cuban exiles escaped a communist regime, many journalists have idealized them as heroes and martyrs of the cold war. A typical article of this genre is found in the *National Geographic Magazine* (July 1973). Entitled "Cuba's Exiles Bring New Life to Miami," the article asserts that the exiles "have prompted many to reexamine a few old values and principles" in the United States. Among those values were the work ethic, pride in one's work, an enterprising spirit, faith in God, respect for the law, family cohesion, self-sacrifice, love for the fatherland, and quest for freedom. According to the *National Geographic*, these qualities explain how a Cuban shoe factory clerk could become a bank president in a few years and how a Cuban exile was able to build the tallest building in Miami. This fabled view emphasizes the virtues of Cuban exiles in light of capitalist ideology in the United States.

The American press tended to praise the Cubans' contributions to the transformation of south Florida from a small tourist area to an important commercial and financial center. Influential magazines such as *U.S. News and World Report, Fortune, Life,* and *Time* recounted the Cuban success story over and over again. The highly touted image of Cuban exiles remained intact until the events surrounding the Mariel boatlift of 1980 recirculated many of the negative stereotypes that the Cuban government cast upon the exiles.[2]

Defenders of the Cuban revolution, on the other hand, emphasized the dark side of the exodus to minimize the importance of those who "voted with their feet" by leaving Cuba. From the triumph of the revolution, particularly after it declared itself Marxist-Leninist, the Cuban government characterized Cuban exiles as *gusanos* (worms). (In 1978 the Cuban government started to use the less charged term "Cuban community abroad" to improve relations with the exiles. In 1994 it held a major conference called "The Nation and Emigration," signaling a major rapprochement with some sectors of the community.)

During the 1960s exiles became objects of public derison in Cuba: their lifestyle was criticized through public speeches, poems, movies, and television. Their values were ridiculed as part of the Cuban state's campaign to create a "new man" in socialist Cuba (see Duany 1979; Lewis et al. 1977–78). Exiles were called *vendepatrias* (antipatriotic sellouts), reactionary, bourgeois, counterrevolutionary, elitists, selfish, and corrupt. In Puerto Rico a local observer described them as follows: "These white and well-dressed refugees, with rings on their fingers, with high positions, and with good cars are the exploiters of always" (Arana-Soto 1963, 249). Although this virulent reaction against Cuban exiles was not typical of all sectors of Puerto Rican society, the stereotype of the arrogant and unscrupulous Cuban took hold in Puerto Rican public opinion.

The Mariel boatlift of 1980 helped recast the negative image of the exiles. The Cuban government referred to the new group of emigrés as *escoria* (scum) and *lumpen* in order to accentuate the presence among them of criminals, homosexuals, and mental patients (see Bach 1982; Clark et al. 1981). The American mass media echoed this image as negative stories about the *Marielitos* began to appear in the *New York Times,* the *Washington Post,* and the *Los Angeles Times* (see Boswell and Rivero 1988). The popular Brian de Palma film *Scarface,* which depicted Cuban exiles as vicious hoodlums, is one of the best-known negative portrayals. In 1982 a Gallup poll showed that Americans perceived Cubans as the second most undesirable group as neighbors in the United States, after members of religious cults (*Miami Herald,* January 21, 1982:15A). The Cuban community in the United States, until then supported by the national press and the federal government, had apparently lost its appeal to American public opinion.

Part of the problem was the vacillation of President Carter during the Mariel crisis. Although the Carter administration initially adopted an open-arms policy toward Cuban exiles, it ended up considering them "entrants" and not refugees.[3] In May 1980 President Carter asserted that the Refugee Law did not apply to Cubans and Haitians who arrived in the United States on boats. This executive decision left the immigrants without a recognized legal status for an indefinite period of time.

The administration not only hesitated about the legal situation of the exiles, but it failed to maintain a coherent policy toward the Cuban government. The only apparent goal of the Carter administration was to embarrass the Castro regime by encouraging people to leave Cuba. As a result, Washington was unable to reach an agreement with Havana to regulate the departure of Cubans. On the contrary, the U.S. government fomented a chaotic situation by allowing Cuban Americans to depart from Key West on boats to pick up relatives and friends (see Clark et al. 1981). President Carter later admitted that the events surrounding the Mariel boatlift contributed to his electoral defeat in 1980. Bill Clinton, then governor of Arkansas, also lost his bid for reelection partly because of the criminal Marielitos sent to his state for imprisonment.

Although this book is not a study of the political ideology of Cuban exiles or of how Cuban exiles are perceived by the American mass media, it is important to correct several erroneous perceptions about the Cuban exodus. The most rigorous studies on Cuban migration do not support the extreme views of the Golden Exile or the dirty worm perspectives. To begin with, the majority of Cuban exiles are not rich, highly educated, or highly skilled. Just as previous immigrants to the United States, Cuban exiles confront multiple problems of adaptation to the new society. Additionally, the exiles are not a collection of immoral sellouts but rather a group of individuals attempting to cope with conditions in their lives in Cuba provoked both by the far-reaching measures of the Cuban revolution and the economic embargo imposed on Cuba by the United States. Finally, it is important to note that the Cuban exodus has not had a homogeneous composition but has followed the changing tide of the Cuban revolution and its relations with the United States. To understand this heterogeneity we need to look at the history of Cuban immigration to the United States and Puerto Rico.

Stages of Cuban Migration

The academic literature divides the Cuban exodus into six or seven stages (Boswell and Curtis 1984, 38–60; Esteve 1984, 25–39; Hernández 1985, 77; Pérez 1986, 129–30; Portes and Bach 1985, 85–86).[4] (See table 2.1 or a summary of the stages of Cuban emigration since 1959.) In this section we follow this precedent and outline the different migration waves from Cuba to the United States during the twentieth century. Focus will be on the migrants' socioeconomic characteristics and settlement patterns.

Table 2.1. Stages of the Cuban exodus to the United States, 1959–1994

Stage	Dates	Important events	No. of emigrants
1. Golden exile	Jan. 1959–Oct. 1962	From triumph of revolution to Cuban Missile Crisis	215,000
2. Clandestine migration /third-country migration	Nov. 1962–Nov. 1965	From Cuban Missile Crisis to Camarioca	74,000
3. Freedom flights	Dec. 1965–Apr. 1973	From Camarioca to end of air bridge	302,000
4. Third-country migration	May 1973–Mar. 1980	From end of air bridge to Mariel boatlift	38,000
5. Freedom Flotilla	Apr.–Sep. 1980	Mariel boatlift	125,000
6. Reduction in migration	Oct. 1980–Nov. 1991	From Mariel boatlift to the economic crisis	121,000
7. The *Balseros* (rafters)	Jan. 1992–Dec. 1994	From the cities to the renegotiation of migration agreements	45,000

The Prerevolutionary Exodus

Prior to 1959 a small but steady number of Cubans migrated to the United States. Cuban immigration to the United States began in earnest in 1868 as a result of the Ten Year War (1868–78) between Cuban insurrectionists and the Spanish government, and it grew with the Cuban Independence War (1895–98). By the 1870s about 12,000 Cubans lived in the United States (Poyo 1991, 24). Mainly as a result of these migratory flows, there were large Cuban immigrant settlements by the beginning of the twentieth century in Key West, Tampa, New York City, and New Orleans. Subsequent crises in the international sugar market and political turbulence in the infant Cuban republic provoked further migration to the United States (Pérez 1978).

Miami, the main port of entry for the refugees, became an important Cuban migration center in the 1930s with the overthrow of the regime of the dictator Gerardo Machado (1924–33) (see Argüelles 1982). During the 1940s and 1950s thousands of Cubans migrated to the United States, especially New York City, searching for better economic opportunities. In 1958 about 40,000 thousand Cubans lived in the United States; most of them were either political refugees or skilled workers in the tobacco industry (Boswell and Curtis 1984, 40–41). While modest, Cuban immigration to the United States had almost a one-hundred-year history before the advent of the Cuban revolution.

From the Golden Exile to the Bay of Pigs

The massive exodus of Cuban exiles began shortly after the collapse of the Batista regime at the end of 1958. The first to leave were military officials, political leaders, state bureaucrats, landowners with extensive property, and business proprietors closely identified with Batista. These initial emigrants were joined shortly afterward by members of the upper middle class, such as professionals, technicians, and managers, who were disillusioned by the leftist turn of the Cuban revolution. Some scholars have described the 1959–62 period as the "Golden Exile" because the vast majority of the refugees originated from the upper stratum of Cuban society (Portes 1969). Several studies of this initial period found that white-collar workers, urban residents, and light-skinned individuals were overrepresented (Cuba, Comité Estatal de Estadísticas 1982; Fagen et al. 1968). These studies also stressed the ideological nature of the motivation of most emigrants, who left Cuba because of political, social, and religious reasons. About one fourth of all

Cuban exiles (approximately 215,000 persons) came to the United States between 1959 and 1962 (Clark 1983, 39).[5]

Until 1961, when the United States and Cuba broke off diplomatic relations, Cubans were able to obtain immigrant visas and travel directly from Havana to Miami. Between 1,600 and 1,700 Cubans arrived weekly in the United States during this period (U.S. Department of Justice 1978, 18). These refugees were principally nuclear families admitted to the United States with temporary visas who applied for refugee status upon arrival. Most never intended to settle permanently in the United States but rather planned to return to Cuba soon, anticipating that Castro's regime would be overthrown. The bulk of the refugees stayed in Miami because of its proximity to Cuba and because this city had become a center of anti-Castro activities. In 1961 the failure of the Bay of Pigs invasion initiated a new era in the Cuban exodus: the revolution was an established fact; exile could no longer be regarded as a transitory status.

Although Cuba and the United States had no diplomatic relations, Cubans were still able to come to the United States on commercial flights until 1962. To be allowed to leave, Cubans had to secure a visa waiver from the U.S. State Department and dollars to purchase the airplane ticket. Both the visa waiver and the dollars were sent by relatives living in the United States.

From the Missile Crisis to Camarioca

The October 1962 missile crisis halted the massive migration of Cubans to the United States. As a consequence, the number of illegal immigrants who arrived in small boats or other makeshift vessels increased significantly. Around 6,700 Cuban exiles arrived in Florida through these means between 1962 and 1965 (Boswell and Curtis 1984, 48; Clark 1983). An additional 56,000 Cubans immigrated to the United States via third countries such as Spain and Mexico.[6] But as a result of the political tensions between Cuba and the United States, commercial flights between both countries ceased until September 1965, when the Cuban government allowed 5,000 Cubans to leave for the United States through the port of Camarioca.

The Freedom Flights

The Camarioca exodus marked the beginning of a new phase in Cuban migration to the United States. Negotiations between Cuba and the United States resulted in the establishment of an aerial bridge, dubbed "Freedom

Flights," that remained in effect between December 1965 and April 1973. Between 3,000 and 4,000 Cuban exiles arrived monthly in the United States on the Freedom Flights (U.S. Department of Justice 1978, 18). This aerial bridge accounted for 302,000 arrivals (Clark 1983, 39), about 35 percent of the Cuban exodus between 1959 and 1991. Since most of the new arrivals were relatives of Cuban exiles, informal social networks played an important part in their adaptation in the United States (Cué and Bach 1980).

By 1973 a change in the composition of the exile population was well under way. Although Cubans from higher socioeconomic strata were still overrepresented, the refugee flux was more diverse than in the past in terms of income, occupation, education, and place of residence. In 1974, while the proportion of professionals and managers declined among the new refugees, more than 41 percent originated from more modest backgrounds, such as salespersons and manual workers (Portes et al. 1977). Like their predecessors, the new immigrants settled mainly in the city of Miami and other parts of Dade County, re-creating their society of origin's heterogeneous class structure. The main destination of most new arrivals reaffirmed a trend that had become evident in the 1960s: Miami had replaced New York City as the leading center of Cuban migration to the United States.

The Freedom Flights ceased in April 1973, and as a result Cuban migration decreased significantly. Only 38,000 Cubans arrived in the United States between 1973 and 1979, mainly from other countries that now included Jamaica and Venezuela (Boswell and Curtis 1984, 50). The diversification of the socioeconomic backgrounds of the exiles continued further. Some authors, such as Bach (1982), argue that economic motives were more important than political reasons during this stage of the Cuban exodus. But as others have indicated, economic and political motives to emigrate are practically inseparable (see Portes and Bach 1985).

The Mariel Boatlift

The dramatic events of the Mariel boatlift, between April and September 1980, received extensive coverage in the American media. Some of the circumstances surrounding the Mariel boatlift are well known in the United States. First, the boatlift was fueled by the visits to Cuba of more than 100,000 Cuban exiles, who made relatives aware of economic opportunities in the United States. Second, Castro, angry at the Peruvian government's refusal to return some Cuban dissidents who crashed through the Peruvian embassy's gates to request political asylum, exhorted all Cubans who were so inclined to go to the embassy and promised no interference from Cuban authorities. Third, fueled by hopes of leaving for the United States, over 10,000 Cubans crowded onto the Peruvian embassy grounds. Fourth, in light of this situation, the Cuban government offered the alternative that Cubans desiring to leave could be picked up at the port of Mariel, near Havana. Fifth, when the exiles arrived on boats at Mariel to pick up their relatives, the Cuban government forced the boats' occupants to transport to the United States unrelated individuals. Some of these persons selected by the Cuban government had been inmates at prisons or mental hospitals.

A less well known fact is that only 2 percent of the Marielitos were common criminals, although as many as 25 percent of the Mariel exiles had been imprisoned in Cuba for a variety of reasons (Clark et al. 1981; cf. Hernández and Gomis 1986). The Mariel boatlift resulted in 124,779 arrivals at Key West, around 14 percent of the total Cuban exodus to the United States. Most of the Marielitos were young men traveling alone. A large proportion were black or mulatto, and many had limited schooling and had been manual workers. The vast majority settled in Dade County, their presence accentuating even more the division between "old" and "new" Cuban exiles.

The 1980s

Cuban migration diminished substantially after 1980 because Cuban entrants ceased to be automatically regarded as political refugees in the United States. Between 1981 and 1991 the U.S. government admitted 154,052 Cuban immigrants (U.S. Department of Justice 1992, table 2), about half as many as in the previous decade. A large number of Cubans are still waiting to join their relatives in the United States, but legal and political issues in both Cuba and the United States have prevented their orderly departure from Cuba. In 1985, in response to the inauguration of U.S.-sponsored Radio Martí, the Cuban government suspended a migratory agreement signed in 1984. During the Reagan presidency, both governments agreed to repatriate Marielitos with criminal records.

Migration to the United States remained a problematic issue between the Cuban and U.S. governments in the 1980s (Bach 1988; Hernández 1985). According to the Cuban government, approximately 40,000 Cubans applied to travel to the United States between 1980 and 1987. In 1987 both governments renewed a bilateral agreement allowing the immigration to the United States of up to 20,000 Cubans per year. In 1989 only 1,850 individuals applied for visas at the U.S. Interests Section in Havana. According to the Interests Section, the majority of Cubans interested in emigrating had left for other countries (Hernández and Azcuy 1990). Other factors that explain the minute number of visa applications are the cumbersome bureaucratic requirements and the potential rejection of visa applicants by the local government and population.

The 1990s

The Cuban exodus increased in the 1990s primarily as a consequence of the deteriorating economic conditions in Cuba. In July 1991 the U.S. State Department announced that it would temporarily stop processing new tourist visa applications in Havana due to a glut of 28,000 applications. In 1990 almost 15,000 of the Cubans who traveled to the United States on tourist visas did not return (*Miami New Herald,* July 30, 1991, 1a, 4a). Additionally, as reported in the American mass media, the number of escapes from Cuba on rafts, makeshift boats, and other unconventional means had soared. In 1991 alone more than 2,000 Cubans escaped to the United States (*El Nuevo Día,* January 26, 1992, 20). These events suggested an increase in pressures to migrate from Cuba to the United States in the early 1990s.

In August 1994 a new cycle in the Cuban exodus took place. The U.S. Coast Guard intercepted over 20,000 Cuban refugees near Florida and relocated them in the naval base in Guantánamo and in the Panama Canal Zone. More than 30,000 Cubans were placed in temporary camps awaiting their legal and administrative processing. President Clinton announced stiffer restrictions on the U.S. embargo on Cuba, including limitations on travel and remittances by Cuban Americans. The Immigration and Naturalization Service declared its plans to exclude Cubans from current refugee programs. Finally, the U.S. and Cuban governments agreed to allow the legal migration of 20,000 Cubans per year, temporarily solving the migration crisis.

To sum up, the Cuban exodus has consisted of several waves over the last three decades. Emigration began among those disaffected with the Cuban revolution, who were found disproportionately in the more advantaged sectors. But subsequent developments in Cuba-U.S. relations as well as deteriorating economic conditions in Cuba resulted in a heterogeneous exile community from different social, economic, and political backgrounds in Cuba (Azicri 1982).

The Socioeconomic Adaptation of Cuban Exiles

Once their historical origins are understood, Cubans' current situation in their new home must be addressed with some caution. The impressive overall statistics pertaining to the Cuban population in the United States hide important internal cleavages. Although many Cubans have succeeded economically in the United States, numerous others have made more-modest achievements. In 1989 the income of one out of every five Cuban families in the United States was below $10,000, and 15 percent lived under the federal poverty line (U.S. Department of Commerce 1991, table 2). In Miami, where half the population of Cuban Americans lived in 1980, just 18 percent of the exiles had well-paying jobs such as managers, professionals, and technicians. More than 53 percent of Cuban Americans in Miami occupied positions in the lower strata, such as operatives, laborers, and service workers (Grenier 1990, 32). These data do not concur with popular stories of universal wealth among Cuban exiles.

On the contrary, many Cubans have experienced a loss of occupational prestige in the United States (Rogg and Cooney 1980). It is not hard to find a Cuban lawyer selling cars in Miami or a certified teacher working at a factory in West New York. Even in the 1970s thousands of Cubans worked in the United States at jobs below their qualifications (Mackey and Beebe

Table 2.2. Occupational distribution of Cuban exiles in the United States, 1990

Occupation	Men	Women
Managers and professionals	25.9	22.1
Technical, sales, and clerical	20.2	47.5
Craftsmen and repairmen	20.9	1.3
Operatives and laborers	20.9	10.4
Service workers	11.3	18.3
Agricultural workers	1.1	0.4
Totals	100.3[b]	100.0

Note: Percent of total employed persons sixteen years of age or older.
[a]Percentages do not add to 100 due to rounding.
Source: U.S. Department of Commerce (1991, table 2).

1977, 30). This phenomenon translates into an enormous waste of human capital. Another sector of the Cuban community that does not fit the Golden Exile image is the elderly. Many do not speak English, have low incomes, and live at the margins of American society. Many aged Cubans form part of a disadvantaged elderly community in Little Havana (Prohías and Casal 1974).

When Mariel refugees are brought into the picture, success stories become more scarce. This immigrant wave consisted of people with less education and fewer occupational skills than earlier immigrants. Many Marielitos looked less like escapees from political oppression and more like traditional immigrants in search of higher standards of living. Even before Mariel, the exile population with lower socioeconomic backgrounds had increased in both relative and absolute terms as a result of continuing economic deprivation and political repression in Cuba (Clark 1990; Portes et al. 1977).

Cuban exiles are well represented at all levels of the American occupational structure except in agricultural and service jobs (see table 2.2). In 1990 Cuban men concentrated in managerial, professional, technical, sales, and skilled occupations. Cuban women were found most frequently in clerical, sales, managerial, and professional occupations.

In sum, Cuban exiles are located throughout the U.S. occupational structure and come from all sectors of Cuban society. This renders strict class interpretations of the exodus grossly inadequate. Retired elderly couples living modestly in Little Havana are as typical of the Cuban community as are well-to-do families living in plush Coral Gables. It is misleading to describe Cuban immigration to the United States and Puerto Rico as an exclusively upper-class phenomenon.

Nonetheless, the exiles' social origins facilitated their incorporation into the American labor market. It is no secret that the exiles overrepresent the upper stratum of prerevolutionary Cuba—the wealthier, better-educated, urban, lighter-skinned, and higher occupational sectors that were alienated by the radical turn of the Cuban revolution in the early 1960s (Casal and Hernández 1975; Fagen et al. 1968; Pérez 1986). Disproportionately large numbers of professionals, managers, clerical and sales employees, and skilled workers settled in the United States and Puerto Rico. The explanation for this selectivity is both economic and political: the revolution waged its income distribution programs largely at the expense of the upper and middle sectors of Cuban society. Those who were most negatively affected were among the first to flee; those who had to gain from social readjustments—

the very poor, the chronically unemployed, isolated peasants, and blacks—usually stayed in Cuba (Amaro and Mesa-Lago 1971).

Upon arrival in America, Cuban exiles were classified by the U.S. government as political refugees.[7] This legal status helped in the social and economic adaptation of Cuban exiles in the United States and Puerto Rico (Pedraza-Bailey 1985). The Cuban Refugee Program, which operated between 1961 and 1974, constituted an exceptional case in the immigration policy of an industrialized country (Amaro and Portes 1972). The federal government assigned over $1 billion to assist the refugees in their occupational, educational, and language needs. In addition to assistance in resettling outside the Miami area,[8] Cuban exiles were offered financial help, scholarships for study, English classes, federal loans, and relaxed requirements for naturalization (Domínguez 1975). For example, the 1966 Cuban Adjustment Act allowed the refugees to obtain permanent residence within a year of arrival and U.S. citizenship five years later. The U.S. government had political as well as humanitarian reasons for instituting these programs; it wanted to show the world that communism was a repressive system and that the exiles were freedom-loving citizens.

The Cuban Refugee Program not only supported the exiles' efforts to achieve economic independence but also promoted their sense of identity as an immigrant group. The U.S. State Department clearly favored Cubans over other immigrants such as Mexicans, Haitians, and Salvadorans (Pedraza-Bailey 1985). Local authorities and citizens reinforced the enthusiastic reception by the federal government, at least in the early 1960s. According to Mackey and Beebe (1977), Miami's citizens not only tolerated Cubans but also supported their cultural singularity. In 1963 Dade County public schools instituted the first bilingual school program in American public education, and in 1973 they proclaimed themselves officially bilingual in English and Spanish.

Over the past two decades attitudes of the local Miami population toward Cuban exiles have deteriorated, particularly after the influx of Marielitos. In 1980 racial conflict between blacks and Hispanics rocked Miami. In an election held a few months later, the citizens of Dade County approved a resolution calling for the retraction of the public schools' bilingual policy and requiring the use of English in educational and cultural activities supported with public funds. Although the vast majority of Miami's non-Hispanic population voted in favor of the resolution, animosity toward Cubans has not reached the levels of anti-Mexican sentiment in the Southwest or anti–Puerto Rican feeling in the Northeast. As Frederickson and Knoble (in Pettigrew et al. 1982, 63) assert, "any prejudice that the Cuban minority may have encountered in South Florida resembles the animus experienced by Jews and Japanese in the United States, which is rooted more in economic jealousy than in lack of respect."[9]

The Acculturation of Cuban Exiles

Whereas the occupational adaptation of early Cuban refugees was essentially unproblematic, their cultural assimilation was not (Portes 1969). In the early 1960s most Cuban exiles saw their migrant condition as transitory: sooner or later the United States would intervene in Cuba, Castro would fall, and Cuban exiles would be able to return. As Fagen, Brody, and O'Leary (1968) put it, Cubans were in exile from the Castro government but not from Cuba itself. Even when their "brief" exile turned into a lengthy stay, most Cubans retained a strong attachment to the homeland. In this respect, early Cubans resemble classic middleman groups, which, as noted in chapter 1, retain a sojourner perspective.

Recently, however, Cuban exiles have begun a transition from political exiles to an ethnic minority. For example, a recent survey conducted by Florida International University among Cuban exiles in Miami found that just 27 percent said that they would return to Cuba if Castro were overthrown (Grenier and Gladwin 1991). Portes attributes this transition to ethnic competition: "It is only when minorities start to abandon their internal colonies, neighborhoods, and enclaves and compete directly with other groups that awareness of racial and cultural differences will be heightened and form the basis for mobilization" (1984, 385).

Cubans in southern Florida are singular in that they have not assimilated culturally but have done well economically. The reason, according to Wilson and Portes (1980), is that Cubans have created an ethnic enclave in Miami. As of 1977 the Miami metropolitan area included 7,336 Cuban-owned firms, mostly in the areas of service, retail trade, and construction (Díaz-Briquets 1984). In 1982 the U.S. census enumerated 20,795 Cuban firms in Dade County (Grenier 1990, 31). As discussed in chapter 1, ethnic enclaves are economically diverse, business-oriented, and relatively independent from the host society. One of their most notable features is that their work conditions fall between the favorable situation enjoyed by large corporations' employees and the adverse circumstances experienced by workers in peripheral businesses that rely largely on minority labor. Moreover, ethnic enclaves foster the immigrants' cultural identity by employing ethnic solidarity as an economic resource.

The experiences of Cuban exiles in the United States defy conventional assumptions about immigrants' adaptation to the host society. Compared with other immigrants in the United States, Cubans are more diverse occupationally, geographically concentrated, and culturally unassimilated. They have developed communities that maintain a strong sense of cultural identity in several American cities. And they have created a solid business sector that will assure the subsistence base of those communities, at least for another generation.

Cuban American Communities: Differences and Similarities

Miami

The roughly 517,000 Cubans living in Miami in 1990 represent about 50 percent of the entire Cuban American population. These statistics make Miami the second largest Cuban city, smaller than Havana but larger than Santiago de Cuba. Cubans in Miami constitute a highly organized community that resists geographical dispersion, even though they have spread out of the Little Havana area into other areas of Dade County. In Dade County, Cubans are highly segregated from other ethnic groups such as Jews, blacks, Puerto Ricans, Mexicans, and Haitians (Boswell and Curtis 1984, 68). Wilson and Portes (1980) associate this residential segregation with the businesses of the ethnic enclave that prefer to hire Cuban employees and serve mainly the needs of the émigré community (see also Portes and Stepick 1993).[10]

Although the exiles' political activities still center on Cuba, such activities are beginning to reflect a growing interest in the United States. In 1978 fewer than half the Cubans in Miami had become American citizens, so Cubans held few elective offices and had little political bargaining power in relation to their numbers. However, in the 1970s more than 178,000 Cubans were naturalized (Portes and Mozo 1985).[11] Once they naturalize and register to vote, Cubans tend to support the Republican Party and its conservative ideology. Cuban exiles have become more organized recently in order to voice their collective interests more effectively; their voice began to have a significant impact on local, state, and national politics in the mid

1970s. In 1975 the city of Sweetwater elected the first Cuban American mayor, Jorge Valdés, and in 1985 Miami elected Xavier Suárez. The same year, Ileana Ros-Lehtinen became the first Cuban American member of the U.S. House of Representatives. More recently, Lincoln Díaz-Balart was also elected to Congress.[12]

The Mariel exodus transformed the Cuban community in Miami. Whereas 96 percent of the exiles identified themselves as white in the 1970 census (Pérez 1980, 257), 20 percent of the Marielitos were black. The occupational structure of Cubans in Miami became even more heterogeneous than before with the arrival of a large number of service and blue collar workers. As a result, Miami's exile community today is more representative of the whole Cuban population. The Mariel exodus also brought new problems. As Clark et al. state, "The sudden influx of more than 85,000 Mariel refugees in the Miami area has created major problems in housing, unemployment, and apparently crime as well" (1981, 12). Additionally, as Portes points out, "The few thousand delinquents and mental patients put by the Cuban government aboard the boats stigmatized not only the entire Mariel exodus, but the pre-Mariel exile population as well" (1984, 394).

West New York and Union City

The second largest concentration of Cubans in the United States, with a population of 100,000 in 1980, is found in the West New York–Union City area of New Jersey. Here, too, the exiles have created a strong ethnic community that protects them from individual and social disorganization (Rogg 1974; Rogg and Cooney 1980). Cubans in New Jersey are better off economically than in Florida, although the former have experienced extensive downward occupational mobility. Most of the exiles are employed in unskilled and blue collar occupations; the majority are factory workers. Many were members of Cuba's lower class, but others were professionals and managers who were forced to accept low-status jobs in the United States. As Prohías and Casal put it, "The high percentage of blue-collar and manual workers in West New York suggests a community in which emigration has meant an even more catastrophic loss of status than for Miami refugees" (1974, 65).

The Cuban community in West New York remains strongly identified with its culture of origin. This allegiance is due largely to the predominance of foreign-born individuals and the proliferation of Cuban organizations in the area. West New York has many Cuban-owned businesses, several newspapers (such as *La Tribuna, El Clarín,* and *Ultima Hora*), a host of church-related voluntary associations, and even right-wing terrorist groups, such as Omega 7. These organizations have slowed down the rate of cultural assimilation to American society. Just as Miami has a Little Havana, West New York has a Little Santa Clara, due to the large number of exiles from this Cuban province.

Other Exile Communities in the United States

Cubans in other cities are more affluent and more acculturated to American society than their counterparts in Miami or West New York. In Milwaukee and Indianapolis most exiles have adjusted well to their new occupations and have recovered the status they had in Cuba (Casal and Hernández 1975; Portes 1969). Cubans average higher incomes, educational levels, and occupational achievements in New York, Illinois, and California than they do in Florida and New Jersey. In 1970 most of New York Cubans lived in upper-middle-class neighborhoods (Cooney and Contreras 1978). Wherever they reside the exiles have limited interaction with other Hispanic groups such as Mexicans, Puerto Ricans, and Dominicans. Cuban exiles are often physically separated from other minorities because Cubans tend to live in suburbs whereas other minorities tend to reside in inner-city areas. But even when they share the same neighborhoods, as is the case in Washington Heights, New York, Cubans and other Hispanics cross national lines primarily in public places such as parks, schools, markets, and churches (Domínguez 1973). Current patterns of social interaction suggest that most Cuban Americans continue to identify themselves on the basis of their national origin rather than on some trait they may share with other groups, such as Spanish-language use.

The persistence of ethnic identity among Cuban exiles can be attributed in part to social networks that extend beyond different states in America. In favoring family reunion, U.S. immigration laws have helped strengthen these networks. Until 1962 Cubans with family members in the United States found it easier than other Cubans to obtain visas to come to this country (Esteve 1984, 30). After 1965 it became easier for Cubans with relatives in the United States to receive political asylum. The Cuban government unwittingly made it easier for Cubans with relatives abroad to emigrate when it began to require that airplane tickets to the United States be purchased with U.S. dollars. Because family networks played such an important part in their migration experience, most Cubans keep in touch with relatives in Cuba, the United States, and Puerto Rico.

Conclusion

Two opposite images—the Golden Exile and the dirty worm—have dominated the academic and popular literature on the Cuban exodus. This chapter presented evidence that contradicts both of these stereotypical views of Cuban migration to the United States. On the one hand, the Golden Exile characterization is appropriate only for the Cuban exodus between 1959 and 1962, when the bulk of the exiles originated from the middle and upper sectors of Cuban society. On the other hand, the dirty worm epithet reflects a simplistic, ideologically rooted condemnation of a highly complex human phenomenon. Popular images aside, in the last three decades Cuban migration to the United States has become increasingly representative of the population of origin, particularly after the Mariel boatlift.

Whether or not the Cuban revolution represented a threat to the life of the exiles, the American government defined them as refugees fleeing political persecution. Like many other diaspora peoples, Cubans left their country because of a perceived threat against their rights. The public reception of Cubans in the United States was generally favorable, at least until the Mariel episode, because the exodus occurred during the cold war and put Cuba, an ally of the Soviet Union, in a negative light. Thus, the U.S. government supported the immigrants' socioeconomic adaptation through the Cuban Refugee Program and other federal policies.

Despite similarities with the experiences of other groups, Cuban immigration history is unique in certain respects. First, returning to the homeland is not a viable alternative for most Cubans, with the consequence that their sojourner outlook is gradually giving way to a settler mentality. Second, the exiles initially did not constitute, on the whole, a displaced peasantry seeking land or a proletariat in search of opportunities. Rather, they were primarily a displaced sector of the urban middle classes. Third, Cubans have succeeded in preserving much of their culture while adapting relatively well to the American economy, especially in Miami.

Nonetheless, the Cuban exodus toward the United States has common features with other migrant flows from the Caribbean. After the Mariel episode, the U.S. government reevaluated its policy toward Cuban immigration, taking into consideration the increasing hostility from U.S. citizens. During the 1980s and 1990s Washington attempted to reduce the migrant flow from Cuba to the United States. This policy shift responded to the growing socioeconomic diversity of the migrant flow and to the weakening of Cuba's strategic position after the end of the cold war.

On the other hand, Cuban migrants share many of the existential dilemmas of other minority groups in the United States, such as resistance to linguistic and cultural assimilation as well as resistance against prejudice and discrimination. Furthermore, Cuban migration has had a strong economic impact on the sending society, similar to other migrant flows from the Caribbean. Finally, the Cuban government has sporadically used immigration to the United States as a safety valve, especially during the Camarioca and Mariel boatlifts and in the 1994 migration crisis.

In closing this chapter, we would like to emphasize that Cubans in Puerto Rico and the United States have followed different modes of economic adaptation. Whereas Cubans in Miami have created an ethnic enclave and Cubans in other cities occupy middle- or high-status jobs in the general economy, exiles in Puerto Rico have played the role of a middleman group. As has been the case in other settings, middleman economic specialization has generated some conflict between the exiles and the receiving society. The following chapter concentrates on ethnic tensions between Cubans and their Puerto Rican hosts.

3

Cuban Migration to Puerto Rico

Compared with the major Cuban communities in the United States, the exile community of Puerto Rico represents a small proportion of the Cuban exodus—between 2 and 3 percent of the exiles in 1990. Around twenty thousand Cubans reside in Puerto Rico, where they function primarily as commercial middlemen in the San Juan area (Cobas 1985). Cubans have invested most of their financial and human capital in retail trade and professional services, working mainly as salespersons, administrators, professionals, and technicians. In this chapter we will outline the current situation of Cubans in Puerto Rico as well as Cuban–Puerto Rican relations in the last three decades.

The Current Situation

The experiences of Cubans in Puerto Rico are different from those of their compatriots in the United States. To begin with, Cubans in Puerto Rico lack the political clout that they have gained in southern Florida as a result of their sheer numbers and formal organization. No Cuban has ever gained a seat in Puerto Rico's legislature. The sole exception to this trend has been at the local level. In 1988 Cuban businessman Reinaldo Castellanos, running on the ticket of the Popular Democratic Party, was elected president of the Municipal Assembly of Carolina, part of the San Juan metropolitan area. Although many exiles are registered with the New Progressive Party, which favors statehood for Puerto Rico, Cubans in Puerto Rico do not constitute a unified voting block. As do many other middleman groups, Cubans in Puerto

Rico represent a visible and economically powerful group that is also politically vulnerable. Like other "pariah capitalists," they do not have direct access to the ruling elite, although some belong to the wealthiest sectors of the host society.

Cuban migration to San Juan was more selective than to American cities (Cooney and Contreras 1978, 47). This selectivity helps explain why Cubans have been far more successful economically in Puerto Rico than in the United States. Casal put it this way: "There are areas, such as Puerto Rico, in which migration biases have produced a concentration of upper-class and upper-middle-class Cubans—entrepreneurs, salesmen, media specialists, and other professionals—who have reestablished and even improved upon their occupational positions in their society of origin" (1979, 119). According to Esteve (1984), the initial migration of Cubans to Puerto Rico was due to the boom of the Puerto Rican economy during the 1960s that resulted from "Operation Bootstrap." Like other middleman groups, Cubans in Puerto Rico found an economically profitable niche in the receiving society.

The difference between Cubans in Puerto Rico and the United States is not just economic but also cultural. As a Cuban clerical worker who participated in Duany's field study said, "since we live in a small island that has roots and a language similar to our own, we Cubans who live in Puerto Rico are developing a 'Cubanness' that is totally different from that of Cubans in Miami and other countries." For example, the out-marriage rates among Cubans are much higher in San Juan than in other cities, such as New York (Fitzpatrick and Gurak 1979). This trait is discussed in chapter 4.

The massive migration of Cubans to Puerto Rico began in the 1960s. In 1940 only 307 Cubans lived in Puerto Rico; in 1960 the number was 538; but by 1970 an estimated 26,000 resided on the island (Vázquez Calzada and Morales del Valle 1979b). The first large-scale movement of Cubans from Miami to San Juan was sponsored by the U.S. Cuban Refugee Program and Puerto Rico's Department of Economic Development during Muñoz Marín's tenure as governor. Cubans arrived at an average annual rate of 3,200 individuals in the early 1960s (González 1970, 27). Most of the exiles arrived during the late 1960s and early 1970s via the Freedom Flights from Varadero to Miami (Esteve 1984). The largest group of Cuban nationals in Puerto Rico ever registered with the U.S. Immigration and Naturalization Service numbered 30,410 persons in 1971 (U.S. Department of Justice 1980). After that the Cuban-origin population stabilized at around 30,000 persons. The 1980 census counted 22,811 Cuban-born individuals (U.S. Department of Commerce 1984a, table 43). An additional 2,000 Mariel exiles relocated to Puerto Rico after 1980 (*El Nuevo Día,* November 29, 1984).[1] By 1990 the census found only 19,736 Cuban-born persons in Puerto Rico (U.S. Department of Commerce 1993, table 4), a figure that suggests a net out-migration of Cubans from Puerto Rico to the United States in the 1980s.

In 1990 more than 85 percent of Puerto Rico's Cuban population resided in the San Juan metropolitan area (U.S. Department of Commerce 1993, table 32). The second largest concentration of Cubans in Puerto Rico (about 4 percent) was in the city of Ponce, and 3 percent lived in Caguas. The rest of the Cuban population was mostly dispersed throughout other major urban centers such as Mayagüez and Arecibo.

Although the Puerto Rican census does not disaggregate data by race, aggregate statistics for the United States reflect the general pattern for Cubans in Puerto Rico. The 1970 census classified the vast majority of Cubans in the United States—95 percent prior to the Mariel exodus—as white (Casal and Hernández 1975). This preponderance of individuals from European backgrounds is just as evident, if not more noticeable, among the exiles in Puerto Rico. Thus, most Cubans live in "white" upper-middle-class neighborhoods such as Torrimar, University Gardens, Isla Verde, Santa Rosa, College Park, and Torremolinos (Cooney and Contreras 1978).

Most Cubans in Puerto Rico come from Havana, Santiago, and other major Cuban cities. A large majority of Duany's informants were born in Havana and Oriente provinces, mainly in their urban centers, a trend also found among respondents in Cobas's survey. Both Duany's and Cobas's data show that before the revolution most respondents concentrated in trade, management, or professional jobs. This business and professional background played an important part in Cubans' economic success in Puerto Rico. Additionally, many exiles had had business relationships with Cuban branches of American banks and, using those connections, were able to obtain loans from the same banks to start businesses in Puerto Rico (Publicidad Badillo 1967). Although many of the exiles initially experienced downward occupational mobility in Puerto Rico, most were able to move up within just a decade. In brief, an important segment of the Cuban petite bourgeoisie reestablished itself in San Juan between 1960 and 1970.

Cuban–Puerto Rican Relations

The historical and cultural links between Cuba and Puerto Rico date back to the Spanish colonial period. The two islands were Spain's remaining two possessions in the Americas after the loss of most of its former colonies in the early nineteenth century. Politically and economically, Cuba and Puerto Rico grew even closer during the second half of the century (see Freire 1966 for an account of the political connections). Many illustrious Puerto Ricans participated in Cuba's wars of independence against Spain, such as Francisco Rius Rivera, Pachín Marín, and Lola Rodríguez de Tió. Puerto Rican intellectuals, including Eugenio María de Hostos, Ramón Emeterio Betances, Sotero Figueroa, and José de Diego, supported the Cuban liberation struggle. The Cuban Revolutionary Party, based in New York, had a Puerto Rican section. Cubans and Puerto Ricans mingled easily in the immigrant communities of New York, New Orleans, Key West, and elsewhere.

After the Spanish-Cuban-American War of 1898, both Cuba and Puerto Rico were occupied militarily by the United States. Although Cuba became an independent republic and Puerto Rico remained a U.S. territory, relations between the two countries continued during the twentieth century. In 1915 de Diego founded a cultural association, Unión Antillana, to promote literary and artistic exchanges among Cuba, Puerto Rico, and the Dominican Republic. More important was the Puerto Rican exodus to Cuba during the first three decades of this century. By 1930 about twenty-five thousand Puerto Ricans were living and working in Cuba, mostly in the sugar plantations of Oriente (Freire 1966). Thus, when Cuban exiles began to emigrate after 1959, many of them had personal contacts with Puerto Ricans, were familiar with Puerto Rican culture, or were aware of the historical affinities with their Spanish Caribbean neighbors.

The 1960s

Relations between Cuban exiles and Puerto Ricans have fluctuated in the last three decades (Borrás 1984; Delgado Imbert 1989). Under the leadership of Gov. Luis Muñoz Marín, Puerto Ricans, in typical fashion, extended their hospitality to Cuban exiles as they began arriving in the 1960s. The exiles received an equally warm welcome from agencies of the federal government in Puerto Rico (Pérez Cruz 1978). But apprehension and resentment began to accumulate as the exiles threatened to displace local workers, particularly the members of the new middle class (Montero Seplowin 1964, 8–12). In 1963 a Puerto Rican writer characterized the exiles as "opportunistic and ungrateful parasites" (Arana-Soto 1963, 301). In a similar vein, the nationalist playwright René Marqués called Cuban exiles "aggressive and without scruples in the struggle for their own survival" (1977, 209). Even Carlos Alberto Montaner, a well-known Cuban exile writer, agreed that "Cuban exiles [in Puerto Rico], besides consciously identifying themselves as strangers, have unconsciously put themselves on the same level with [Puerto Rico's] white and rich elite (*blanquitos y riquitos*)" (1971, 7).

The influx of thousands of Cubans to Puerto Rico was bound to result in conflict because foreign immigration to the island is not regulated by the Puerto Rican government but by the U.S. Immigration and Naturalization Service. Montero Seplowin (1964) found that poor Puerto Ricans did not resent Cubans. However, Safa argued that the members of the urban lower classes thought that Cuban exiles were "arrogant and difficult to deal with as employers and business owners" (1974, 100). In addition, members of Puerto Rico's petite bourgeoisie looked askance at Cuban exiles, with whom they competed in many areas of the economy.

In 1965–66 a public controversy culminated in two major studies of the impact of Cuban immigration into Puerto Rico. The first of these was sparked off by an advertisement in a local newspaper requesting Cuban salespersons.[2] The alleged discriminatory Cuban hiring practices reached both the Senate and the House of Representatives in Puerto Rico. Resolutions were passed to investigate the "unfavorable effects" of foreign immigration (a euphemism for Cuban immigration) on the "well-being and happiness of Puerto Ricans" (House Resolution 125, September 17, 1965).[3] The second study, conducted by the Puerto Rican Bar Association (González 1970), concluded that legal action should be taken to "protect" the natives from unfair competition by foreigners (again, a euphemism), particularly those in professional and semiprofessional occupations. This proposal, however, was never implemented because, among other reasons, commonwealth authorities have no jurisdiction on immigration matters.

Shortly after the discussion of these issues in the local press, Cuban activist Manolo Ray wrote to the San Juan *Star* (September 23, 1965) to explain that "Cuban workers came to fill existing gaps in the demand for skilled personnel in Puerto Rico," not to take away anyone's job. To defend the Cuban community, a group of exiles associated with the Centro Cubano de Puerto Rico commissioned a study on the subject that was carried out by the advertising agency Publicidad Badillo. The study concluded that, rather than depressing salaries on the island (a complaint commonly voiced against Cubans), the influx of Cubans had created new sources of wealth in Puerto Rico. In 1966 even the pro-American San Juan *Star* remarked that "The so-called Cuban problem has been festering in many areas of Puerto Rican life" (March 24, 1966). Cuban writer Carlos Alberto Montaner acknowledged that "foreigners are a constant source of irritation to a growing number of Puerto Ricans" (1971, 7).

The 1970s

Cuban–Puerto Rican relations reached their most critical point in 1972. As the San Juan *Star* put it: "A rumor swept Puerto Rico last November that unless all Cuban exiles left the island by the end of that month, anything could happen. Anonymous threats were mailed to many prominent Cubans and publicized in newspapers. But nothing happened" (March 23, 1973).

The so-called *Comandos anticubanos* were only a small band of extremists, but they expressed a widespread feeling of hostility. Even conservative Puerto Ricans began to protest that they were becoming strangers in their own land. Cuban jokes began to circulate: Question: "En qué se parecen los cubanos a Dios?" (What do Cubans and God have in common?) Answer: "En que están en todas partes y nadie los puede ver" (In that they are everywhere and nobody can "see" [which also means "stand"] them). Other jokes with an abundance of scatological language rose around the topic of Cuban arrogance, ambition, and aggressiveness. A local television comedian, José Miguel Agrelot, became famous for his impersonation of a pushy Cuban exile, Pancho Matanzas. The suspicious attitude of many Puerto Ricans tainted the public image of Cuban exiles.

Even though Ray persisted in his opinion that Cubans had not displaced Puerto Ricans from their jobs, he failed to change public opinion (see *Avance*, January 31, 1973). In the 1970s thousands of Cubans decided to leave Puerto Rico because of Puerto Rican animosity, because the Partido Independentista Puertorriqueño began to voice a rhetoric similar to that of the Cuban revolution, and because the exiles disliked the newly elected governor on the Partido Popular Democrático's ticket, whom they suspected of being procommunist. At the same time, Puerto Rico's "economic miracle" began to fade away, and the island stopped being a showcase for American-style democracy. In addition, the 1970s saw a massive return migration of Cubans from all parts of the United States to Miami. In 1990, 55 percent of Cuban exiles resided in southern Florida, 13 percent more than in 1970 (*The Economist*, September 14, 1991, 31). Many Cubans in Puerto Rico enthusiastically joined the return wave to Miami. Between 1970 and 1980 Puerto Rico lost around three thousand Cuban exiles, most of whom moved to the United States. Today Miami has a small settlement of Cuban exiles who moved from Puerto Rico, some of whom have retired and live in Little Havana.

Cuban–Puerto Rican relations deteriorated as a consequence of two socioeconomic factors: the rapid upward mobility of the exiles and the scarcity of new jobs in Puerto Rico since the 1970s. As a writer stated in the newspaper *El Mundo:*

> Every day more Puerto Ricans come to resent the foreign "invasion." This concern is found in many of the letters we receive daily, in which citizens complain that conditions of high unemployment and lack of jobs faced by Puerto Ricans are aggravated when thousands and thousands of foreigners that come to compete in the job market are admitted into the island. (April 18, 1980)

Population growth in Puerto Rico intensified the effect of the economic crisis, forcing many unemployed Puerto Ricans to move to the United States and making foreigners more visible. Cubans in Puerto Rico, however, were not affected as deeply. As a Puerto Rican demographer states, "Ten years after the arrival of their first wave, Cuban exiles hold the best jobs [and] experience practically no unemployment" (Pérez Cruz 1978, 89). This relatively privileged situation did not help the exiles' popularity.

In addition to their economic prosperity, Cubans exhibited a strong sense of in-group solidarity, despite their being a small and dispersed community throughout the island. Many Puerto Ricans who were preoccupied with their own national identity took umbrage with Cubans' ethnic solidarity. In a clear allusion to Cuban exiles, Puerto Rican writer Salvador Tió reflected this perspective:

> Puerto Rico, a cultural entity, is deeply offended by the isolation of any ethnic group. It wants to ensure that all of those who have settled here will eventually feel and become Puerto Ricans. And even though those who do not assimilate may play very important roles in business and industry, they will not count very much in our political and cultural life. (*El Nuevo Día,* July 4, 1984)

In more dramatic tones, a reader of *El Mundo* wrote that he "was very concerned by the catastrophe that threatens Puerto Rico. Puerto Rican national identity is on the verge of disappearing, because in ten years the island will be inundated with foreigners" (April 18, 1980).

The 1980s

The year 1980 witnessed another dramatic episode between Cubans and Puerto Ricans as a consequence of the Mariel boatlift. While the Cuban community in Puerto Rico opened its arms to the new arrivals, most Puerto Ricans closed theirs. Tensions mounted as preparations were undertaken at the U.S. Army base of Fort Allen, in the town of Juana Díaz, to receive Mariel exiles. Various sectors of Puerto Rican society publicly protested against the plan; no one seemed to want a detention camp on the island (see Esteve 1984, 38–39). Even then Gov. Romero Barceló—a staunch supporter of the Cuban community—opposed the move: 1980 was an election year and the Marielitos could not vote. Cuban groups such as the Unión de Cubanos en el Exilio were left practically alone to welcome the refugees. Once again the whole question of control over immigration surfaced as a sore point between Cubans and Puerto Ricans.

The year 1984 was significant in Cuban–Puerto Rican relations for two unrelated events: the pope's visit and local elections for governor. The pope's words during Mass in San Juan rang clearly in the exiles' ears:

> I can only send a cordial greeting to the Christian brethren who live in this land: the Haitians, those who come from various nations in Europe, the members of other national groups, particularly the numerous believers from Cuba. That name that I have just uttered—Cuba—so close geographically, provokes in me a profound feeling of affection. To all the children of that noble land, priests, seminarians, laymen, Christians of the Pearl of the Caribbean, goes my greeting.

This last phrase—"the Pearl of the Caribbean"—unleashed passionate debates as to which island was the true Pearl, Cuba or Puerto Rico. Many Puerto Ricans felt offended, while Cuban exiles were proud that the pope had singled them out as a special people. The local press speculated that the pope wanted to visit Cuba and that his words reflected his intention to fight against the growth of communism in Latin America.

Election years are particularly tense for Cubans in Puerto Rico because the "foreign issue" is resurrected. One of the sources of strain in the election year of 1984 was the active participation of some Cuban exiles in the political campaign of the Partido Nuevo Progresista, which favors statehood for Puerto Rico. A well-known Cuban actress, Ofelia D'Acosta, received death threats. A letter to *El Nuevo Día* from a procommonwealth Puerto Rican asked Cubans to "go to Miami where there are thousands of other Cubans who want to be American" (October 2, 1984). Some Cubans responded with the formation of a Cuban committee in solidarity with the Partido Popular Demócrata and its candidate for mayor of San Juan, Victoria Muñoz Mendoza, daughter of Luis Muñoz Marín. The committee's organizer underscored the exiles' debt to Muñoz Marín, who "opened up the arms of Puerto Rico for Cubans" (*El Nuevo Día,* October 24, 1984). The committee consisted largely of Cuban liberals—mostly professors, intellectuals, and professionals—who opposed independence as strongly as statehood because "Under the Commonwealth Cubans were able to educate their children, make their homes, establish their businesses, and many have deservedly been able to accumulate fortunes in peace and tranquility" (*El Nuevo Día,* November 3, 1984).

The 1990s

In the 1990s the main political dilemma in Puerto Rico has been the final determination of the island's political status through a plebiscite. The possibility of a plebiscite has been another source of Cuban–Puerto Rican tensions, because many Puerto Ricans feel that Cubans, even those who hold American citizenship, should not be eligible to vote in such an election. Some political commentators argue that, like the French in Algeria and Spaniards in Spanish Morocco, Cubans in Puerto Rico should not participate in the decolonization process. An editorial in *El Mundo* echoed this concern: "Many Puerto Ricans are worried that, when the moment to make a permanent decision on the island's political status, foreigners, persons not born here, people who are not Puerto Rican, will become a decisive force in a monumental decision that belongs to Puerto Ricans and only to Puerto Ricans" (April 18, 1980).

The 1990s have witnessed a renewed political activism in the Cuban community. Political changes in Eastern Europe and the former Soviet Union fanned hopes for democratic change in Cuba. Cuban and Puerto Rican entrepreneurs plan to invest in Cuba's economic reconstruction. Some Cuban exiles have expressed an interest in returning to their homeland, while others plan to remain in Puerto Rico and visit Cuba frequently. Should Castro's government fall, Cuban migration to the United States and Puerto Rico will probably increase. Regardless of the outcome, political events in Cuba will have a significant impact on Puerto Rico's Cuban community.[5]

Conclusion

Cuban migration to Puerto Rico and the United States differs substantially. First, a small segment of the Cuban exodus settled in Puerto Rico, particularly in the San Juan metropolitan area, and specialized in trade, management, and the professions, whereas in Florida, Cubans are far more numerous and more occupationally differentiated. Second, Cubans in Puerto Rico have not achieved the same degree of political power gained by their counterparts in Florida. Third, Cubans in Puerto Rico have encountered fewer cultural, linguistic, and religious differences than in the United States. Fourth, Cubans in Puerto Rico come from higher socioeconomic backgrounds than Cubans in Miami, West New York, and other American cities.

The history of Cuban–Puerto Rican relations in the last three decades has been complex. The exiles' initial reception in Puerto Rico was positive. But economic competition and political differences between segments of the Cuban and Puerto Rican communities generated antagonism toward the exiles. Since the 1960s foreign migration to Puerto Rico has been a controversial issue in light of its potential impact on the job market and local elections. The Cuban community still arouses strong reactions from the local society, as demonstrated by the debate on whether residents of Puerto Rico who are American citizens but were born outside Puerto Rico (primarily Cubans and Dominicans) should be eligible to vote on a plebiscite concerning Puerto Rico's ultimate political status.

As will be discussed in the next chapter, the ambivalent response of Puerto Rican society toward Cubans is one of many characteristics that exiles share with other middleman groups. Many exiles had business backgrounds or experience in Cuba. Particularly in the early years of the revolution, many were sojourners who planned to return to their homeland. Cubans who migrated to Puerto Rico were more representative of the propertied classes than those who migrated to the United States. As will be shown in the next chapter, Cubans specialized in trade and akin activities and dominated some business lines. Like other middleman groups, Cubans in Puerto Rico are almost exclusively urban residents. In the following chapter we will discuss in greater detail these and other characteristics that make Cubans in Puerto Rico fit the middleman group profile.

4

Cubans in Puerto Rico as a Middleman Group

Chapter 1 discussed the characteristics of middleman groups. In this chapter we will demonstrate that the middleman group literature can also aid understanding of the experiences of Cuban exiles in Puerto Rico, particularly in three respects: their socioeconomic profile, their reliance on the in-group for business purposes, and the reactions they have aroused from the Puerto Rican community.

Cubans' Socioeconomic Profile

Vázquez Calzada and Morales del Valle (1979b) used data from the 1960 and 1970 censuses to compare members of different nationalities in Puerto Rico. They showed that Cubans enjoyed higher incomes, higher levels of education, and more prestigious occupations than Puerto Ricans, North Americans, and Dominicans. Data from the 1980 and 1990 censuses are in line with Vázquez Calzada and Morales del Valle's conclusions. In 1979 the median household income for Cubans ($12,290) was more than twice as high as that of Puerto Ricans ($5,348). Median years of education for Cubans and Puerto Ricans were 12.2 and 8 respectively (U.S. Department of Commerce 1984b, tables 95a, 95b). In 1990 the mean household income for Cubans ($31,300) was more than double the mean household income for Puerto Ricans ($14,523) and exceeded the mean household income ($26,943) for persons born in the United States not of a Puerto Rican parent (Rivera-Batiz and Santiago 1996, table 6.3). The same year 37.8 percent of Cubans twenty-five years of age or older had completed college, compared with 13.1 percent among Puerto Ricans (Rivera-Batiz and Santiago 1996, table 6.8). In sum, Cubans in Puerto Rico enjoy high income and educational attainments.

Table 4.1 compares the 1980 occupational characteristics of Cubans and Puerto Ricans on the island. Cubans showed a higher concentration in the managerial and sales occupations than did Puerto Ricans, while Puerto Ricans evinced higher proportions of service workers, farmers, and laborers. Data from the 1990 census show similar trends. As table 4.2 shows, Cubans had higher concentrations in managerial and professional occupations and in technical and sales jobs than did others. In brief, Cubans in Puerto Rico fit the occupational characteristics of middleman groups.

As do other middleman groups, Cubans in Puerto Rico specialize in the provision of goods and services. This propensity was evident in the 1970 census, which showed that Cubans concentrated in the tertiary sector of the

Table 4.1. Occupational characteristics of employed Puerto Ricans and Cubans sixteen years of age and older, Puerto Rico, 1980 (percentages of total)

	Place of birth	
Occupation	Puerto Rico	Cuba
Executive, administrative, and managerial	7.9	15.7
Professionals	11.6	9.8
Technicians	2.0	1.2
Sales	9.4	32.7
Administrative support	14.7	15.4
Service	14.9	7.0
Farming, forestry, and fishing	3.7	0.7
Precision production, crafts	12.8	8.3
Operators and laborers	23.0	9.2
Totals	100.0	100.0

Source: U.S. Department of Commerce (1980b, tables 95a and 95b).

Table 4.2. Occupational distribution of the Puerto Rican population, by navity, 1990 (percentages of total)

	Place of birth			
Occupation	Puerto Rico	Cuba	Dominican Republic	Continental U.S.
Managerial and professional	19.2	36.2	13.4	21.6
Technical, sales, and admin. support	27.9	42.7	23.9	38.0
Service	15.8	5.9	31.4	12.6
Farming, forestry, and fishing	3.3	1.6	1.5	1.2
Precision production, craft, and repair	12.0	8.5	13.5	9.9
Operators, fabricators, and laborers	21.8	5.1	16.4	16.8
Totals	100.0	100.0	100.0	100.0

Source: Special tabulations provided by Carlos E. Santiago.

economy (70 percent), principally in trade (37 percent) (see table 4.3). Cubans had penetrated economic sectors such as construction, advertising, insurance, real estate, restaurants, cafeterias, clothing retail stores, supermarkets, car dealerships, jewelry stores, publishing, and sale of electronic equipment (*El Mundo,* August 8, 1986; Pérez Cruz 1978; Publicidad Badillo 1967). Moreover, Cubans were well represented in the mass media (radio, newspapers, and television) as well as in the independent professions (particularly medicine and engineering). Data from the 1990 census (see table 4.4) show that almost half of the Cuban respondents were located in the trade and finance sectors.

Another characteristic of the Cuban community is a high proportion of individuals who work for themselves. The 1980 census shows that, among employed Cuban respondents at least sixteen years old, 15.5 percent were self-employed. The comparable figure for the rest of the population was 10.4 percent (U.S. Department of Commerce 1984b, table 95b). According to the 1990 census 26 percent of Cubans were self-employed, which was

Table 4.3. Economic sector distribution for Cubans and Puerto Ricans in Puerto Rico, 1970

Economic sector	Cubans	Puerto Ricans
Agriculture and mining	0.3	9.4
Manufacture	12.2	20.0
Construction	11.5	12.2
Transporation and communication	5.6	8.4
Trade	36.9	15.9
Finance	5.2	2.3
Public administration	3.5	7.9
Professional services	12.6	14.8
Personal services	7.0	5.4
Other services	5.2	3.7
Totals	100.0	100.0

Note: Percentages of total, employed persons fourteen years of age and over.
Source: Vázquez Calzada and Morales del Valle (1979b, table 16).

Table 4.4. Economic sector distribution for Puerto Rico, by nativity, 1990 (percentages of total)

	Place of birth			
Economic sector	Cuba	Puerto Rico	Dominican Republic	Continental U.S.
Agriculture and mining	1.9	4.0	1.5	1.5
Manufacture	10.1	17.5	11.5	18.9
Construction	5.4	8.6	11.3	5.2
Transportation and communication	4.5	6.1	4.0	6.2
Trade	41.6	19.6	29.8	25.1
Finance, insurance, real estate	5.9	3.5	2.3	4.2
Public administration	3.5	14.6	5.3	11.3
Services	27.1	26.2	34.2	27.7
Totals	100.0	100.0	100.0	100.0

Source: Tabulations provided by Carlos Santiago.

almost three times the average in Puerto Rico (special tabulation provided by Carlos E. Santiago).

Data from the Cobas survey provides more detailed information. He found that 49.5 percent of respondents were self-employed.[1] As table 4.5 shows, retail merchants comprised 27.8 percent of the self-employed. Another 11.1 percent were salesmen, and an additional 6.5 percent were wholesale merchants. These figures indicate that nearly half of the self-employed were traders. Independent professionals (such as physicians, attorneys, and accountants) and other businessmen accounted for more than one third of the self-employed. Insurance agents and brokers, contractors, and mechanics and artisans accounted for approximately an additional 17 percent. The self-employed included just one farmer.

Among respondents working for others, Cubans tend to be employed in Cuban-owned firms or other foreign businesses, such as North American and Spanish firms. As table 4.6 indicates, 40.9 percent of the respondents in the Cobas study worked in establishments owned either entirely by Cubans or jointly by Cubans and non-Cubans. An additional 30.9 percent were employed in American-owned firms or other foreign firms. Only 28.2 percent worked in Puerto Rican–owned concerns. In brief, Cubans concen-

Table 4.5. Types of economic activity among self-employed Cubans in San Juan

Types	N	%
Independent insurance agent, broker	7	6.5
Retail merchant	30	27.8
Wholesale merchant	7	6.5
Construction contractor	5	4.6
Independent professional	20	18.5
Salesperson	12	11.1
Businessperson	20	18.5
Mechanic, artisan	6	5.6
Farmer	1	0.9
Totals	108	100.0

Source: Authors' survey.

Table 4.6. Ethnicity of owners of businesses in which Cubans in San Juan work (employees only)

Type of employment	N	%
Businesses owned entirely by Cubans	38	34.5
Businesses jointly owned by Cubans and non-Cubans	7	6.4
U.S.-owned businesses	23	20.9
Other non–Puerto Rican owned firms	11	10.0
Puerto Rican–owned concerns[a]	31	28.2
Totals	110	100.0

[a]Includes employees of the Commonwealth of Puerto Rico.
Source: Authors' survey; two cases deleted due to missing data.

trate in their own ethnic economy and other foreign-owned businesses.

In sum, Cubans' median income and educational attainment are higher than those of Puerto Ricans. Cubans are underrepresented in low-level occupations, such as service work and manual labor, and overrepresented in executive, administrative, and managerial positions. Almost a third of all Cubans are in sales occupations, compared to about one tenth of Puerto Ricans. Many Cubans work for themselves; almost half of these are traders. Finally, Cubans who work for others tend to be employed in Cuban-owned or other foreign businesses. A relatively advantaged socioeconomic status, a concentration in sales and trade, and a high proportion of individuals who work for themselves, a coethnic, or a foreign-owned concern are characteristics associated with a middleman group. Thus, the socioeconomic profile of Cubans in Puerto Rico is typical of middleman groups.

Middleman Group Businesses

Middleman group enterprises typically rely on the in-group for resources such as loans and information on business opportunities and depend on cheap coethnic labor. Middleman businesses are often found in undesirable areas. They dominate some business lines, serve an out-group clientele, and tend to be spatially dispersed throughout the host society. In general, Cuban businesses in Puerto Rico conform to these characteristics.

Unfortunately, we do not have much data on sources of capital or the formation of Cuban businesses in Puerto Rico. According to a study conducted by Publicidad Badillo (1967) in the early 1960s, the majority of Cuban businesses in Puerto Rico were established with loans obtained from banks and businesses. These were banks and businesses with which the exiles had dealt before their departure from Cuba. Another study, the Cobas survey, provides evidence that entrepreneurs rely on the in-group to find business partners. Exactly half of the 108 self-employed respondents in the survey were members of business partnerships. Table 4.7 details the ethnic composition of those partnerships. Observe that the vast majority, 70.4 percent, were in all-Cuban partnerships. An additional 20.4 percent were in partnerships involving Cubans and non-Cubans. Only 9.2 percent had exclusively non-Cuban partners.

Although many Cubans work for a coethnic, in the typical Cuban business the majority of employees are out-group members. According to the Cobas survey, the median percentage of Cuban personnel in Cuban enterprises was 29.5 percent, indicating a heavy use of local workers. One reason for this trend is an insufficient supply of working-class Cubans in Puerto Rico. But the importance of Cuban employees in Cuban firms is more than numerical. Table 4.8 details the occupations of the thirty-eight respondents employed in Cuban businesses. Note that about 74 percent were traveling sales representatives, managers, foremen, executives, and accountants. Most of these jobs require trust on the part of the owner, and some represent key

Table 4.7. Ethnic composition of business partnerships of Cubans in San Juan

Ethnic composition	N	%
All Cuban	38	70.4
Mixed[a]	11	20.4
Non-Cuban	5	9.2
Totals	54	100.0

[a]Cubans and non-Cubans.
Source: Authors' survey.

Table 4.8. Cuban business employees in San Juan: detailed occupations

Occupation	N	%
Accountant	2	5.3
Manager	9	23.8
Executive	2	5.3
Cashier	1	2.6
Office clerk	1	2.6
Traveling salesman	13	34.2
Real estate agent	1	2.6
Sales clerk	3	7.9
Foreman	2	5.3
Cannery worker	1	2.6
Plastic maker	1	2.6
Road machine operator	1	2.6
Unclassifiable	1	2.6
Totals	38	100.0

Source: Authors' survey.

positions. In other settings in-group members constitute the major source of labor for middleman businesses. Cuban employees in Puerto Rico perform an equally important function: filling positions of trust.

Little information exists on whether Cubans dominate some business lines. However, there is some evidence that Cubans concentrate in such lines as food retailing and mass communication (Carr 1984; Esteve 1984; Maldonado Denis 1972). Concerning the composition of their clientele, Cuban businesses rely mostly on out-group patronage. The number of Cubans in Puerto Rico is insufficient to support firms oriented exclusively to the Cuban community. As for spatial concentration, San Juan has no Little Havana such as Miami's. Although some areas of the city, such as Río Piedras, have pockets of Cuban businesses, most Cuban businesses are scattered throughout the San Juan metropolitan area. Finally, Cuban businesses do not concentrate in blighted areas but are found in poor as well as more-desirable sections. In this last respect, Cuban businesses do not conform to the typical middleman profile.

Attachment to the In-group

Middleman group members are attached to the in-group. They prefer to interact with and marry coethnics. They strive to maintain their own culture and traditions. As we will show later, Cubans in Puerto Rico are not as clannish as other middleman groups. However, they retain a strong sense of solidarity and ethnic identity. For instance, there are numerous Cuban social and professional organizations in Puerto Rico. The most prominent is the Círculo Cubano de Puerto Rico, popularly known as "Casa Cuba." This and other Cuban organizations are discussed in chapters 6 and 7.

Twenty-six percent of the respondents in the Cobas survey and 32 percent of individuals in Duany's field study belonged to one or more exile organizations. Cobas's figures probably underestimate the degree of voluntary association participation among Cubans in Puerto Rico. Duany's field study shows that voluntary association participation is higher among women, and Cobas's sample included only men. Nevertheless, putting together data from both studies, most Cubans are not actively involved in Cuban voluntary associations.

Table 4.9. Proportion of close friends who are Cuban among Cubans in San Juan

Category	N	%
Less than 10%	31	14.2
10–19%	9	4.1
20–29%	17	7.7
30–39%	5	2.3
40–49%	1	0.5
50–59%	56	25.6
60–69%	9	4.1
70–79%	10	4.5
80–89%	14	6.4
More than 90%	67	30.6
Totals	219	100.0

Source: Authors' survey. One case excluded due to missing data.

Table 4.9 summarizes the distribution of responses to the question in Cobas's survey, "What proportion of your close friends are Cuban?" The median value in this distribution was 57.8 percent, indicating that for half of the respondents at least fifty-eight out of every one hundred friends were coethnics. Duany's field data suggest a similar trend regarding ritual kin (*compadres*). His data further showed that while many Cubans have friendships with Puerto Ricans, most have a circle of close Cuban friends. In sum, Cubans in Puerto Rico show a moderate inclination to maintain close friendships and ritual kin relations within the in-group.

Answers to two other questions in the Cobas survey also failed to show a high degree of in-group attachment. Tables 4.10 and 4.11, respectively, show responses to two attitudinal questions: (1) "Suppose you (or your son) were looking for a young woman to marry. How important would it be to you that the young woman were Cuban?" and (2) "Suppose you were thinking to start a business for which you needed a partner. How important would it be to you that the partner be Cuban?" Concerning the Cuban marriage partner, 67.8 percent said that it was not important, compared with 10.9 percent who asserted that it was very important. Regarding a business partner, 61.2 percent stated that it was not important that the partner be Cuban, which contrasts with only 11.7 percent who said that it was very important.

Marriage data evince moderate in-group attachment. Duany (1985b, ch. 6) studied Cuban marriages in San Juan for four randomly selected years between 1970 and 1983. Table 4.12 shows that Cubans tend to be exoga-

Table 4.10. Responses by by Cubans in San Juan to the question: "Suppose you (or your son) were looking for a young woman to marry. How important would it be to you that the young woman were Cuban?"

Category	N	%
Not important	143	67.8
A little important	26	12.3
Fairly important	19	9.0
Very important	23	10.9
Totals	211	100.0

Source: Authors' survey. Nine cases excluded due to missing data.

Table 4.11. Responses of Cuban exiles in San Juan to the question: "Suppose you were thinking of starting a business for which you needed a partner. How important would it be to you that the partner were Cuban?

Category	N	%
Not important	131	61.2
A little important	38	17.8
Fairly important	20	9.3
Very important	25	11.7
Totals	214	100.0

Source: Authors' survey. One case excluded due to missing data.

Table 4.12. Distribution of Cuban marriages in San Juan, 1970–1983, by nationality and sex

Nationality of marriage partner	Men	Women
Cuban	406 (36.2%)	406 (42.2%)
Puerto Rican	563 (51.5%)	379 (40.6%)
Other[a]	123 (11.2%)	157 (16.8%)
Totals	1092 (100.0%)	932 (100.0%)

[a]Includes Dominicans, Puerto Ricans, Spaniards, Latin Americans, and other foreigners. *Source:* Duany (1985, chap. 6).

mous. During the years selected, the proportion of out-group marriages among Cubans was about 63 percent for the men and 57 percent for the women.[2] If this tendency continues, Cubans will begin to disappear as a distinct ethnic group in the next generation.

Nevertheless, Cubans in Puerto Rico retain a sense of group identity. Three out of five respondents in Duany's fieldwork identified themselves as Cuban, while a small minority saw themselves as Puerto Rican (see table 4.13). Another small proportion felt themselves to be North American or

Table 4.13. Self-ascribed nationality and citizenship of Cubans in San Juan

Country	Self-ascribed nationality	Citizenship
Cuba	56 (58.9%)	25 (26.6%)
Puerto Rico	7 (7.4%)	—
United States	4 (4.2%)	68 (72.3%)
Other countries[a]	28 (29.5%)	1 (1.1%)
Totals	95 (100.0%)	94 (100.0%)

[a]Includes Spain and various combinations.
Source: Authors' study. Five cases were excluded from the first column and six from the second because of missing data.

another foreign nationality. One of four had mixed feelings about his or her national identity, particularly the younger ones. On the other hand, almost three fourths of Duany's sample were U.S. citizens. These data suggest that Cubans in Puerto Rico distinguish clearly between their ethnic identity and their U.S. citizenship. Additionally, Cubans maintain an attachment to the homeland. As we will see in chapter 6, many Cuban voluntary associations in Puerto Rico promote Cuban traditions.

In light of the preceding data, it appears that Cubans are not as clannish as other middleman groups. Cubans exhibit a moderate degree of in-group attachment and are relatively open to members of the host society. However, these data need to be qualified by an important fact: Cubans associate principally with the upper-middle stratum of Puerto Rican society. At least that is the trend in out-group marriages (Duany 1985b, ch. 6). The same propensity applies to other forms of association, such as the voluntary groups discussed in chapter 7.

Puerto Rican Reactions Toward Cuban Exiles

As stated in chapter 3, Puerto Rican reactions to Cuban immigration have been ambivalent. On the one hand, some sectors of Puerto Rican society have given the exiles a warm reception. Cuban entrepreneurs have prospered in Puerto Rico in the last three decades. On the other hand, Cubans have aroused antagonism among other Puerto Ricans. The early 1960s issues of the now defunct daily *El Mundo* are replete with complaints of unfair competition on the part of Cubans. The late Puerto Rican playwright René Marqués dubbed Cuban exiles a "civil corps of espionage, denunciation, and pressure . . . against Puerto Ricans" (1977, 213).

The ambivalence of the host society conforms to the experiences of middleman groups. Middleman groups have friends as well as enemies in the host society. Esteve's study (1984, 87–88) suggests that Puerto Ricans perceive Cubans as hardworking, intelligent, respectful, and likable. But her subjects also perceive Cubans as being selfish, indiscreet, proud, and self-seeking. The image of the Cuban in Puerto Rico coincides with middleman group stereotypes found around the world (Pettigrew et al. 1982, 11).

Table 4.14 reports data from Cobas's survey on Cubans' perception of hostility among Puerto Ricans toward Cubans. Very few found a lot of hostility; the prevalent feeling among respondents is a small or moderate degree of hostility. Animosity on the part of Puerto Ricans seems to be a minor problem for the majority of Cuban exiles in Puerto Rico. Duany's study found that just one third of the respondents admitted being discriminated against because of their nationality. It would seem that Puerto Rican hostility toward Cubans does not result in a strong rejection.

Hostility against Cubans in Puerto Rico is based on three primary sources. First, Cubans are seen as braggarts who harbor a "cultural prejudice against Puerto Ricans" (Lewis 1974, 19). In particular, Cubans tend to see Puerto Ricans as lazy, passive, dependent, submissive, and resigned (Duany 1985b, ch. 5).

Table 4.14. Responses of Cuban exiles in San Juan to the question: "In your view, how much hostility toward Cubans is there in Puerto Rico?"

Category	N	%
A lot	4	1.9
A fair amount	30	14.2
A little	123	58.3
None	54	25.6
Totals	211	100.0

Source: Authors' survey.

Table 4.15. Responses of Cuban exiles in San Juan to the question: "Which political party would you prefer to be in power?"

Party	N	%
Partido Nuevo Progresista (PNP)	137	67.2
Partido Popular Democrático (PPD)	19	9.3
Undecided	5	2.4
Not in favor of any one party	43	21.1
Totals	204	100.0

Source: Authors' survey. Sixteen cases excluded due to missing data.

Second, Cubans are perceived as taking jobs from Puerto Ricans (Lewis 1974, 17–18; Maldonado Denis 1972, 181; Marqués 1977, 209). Although competition over jobs occurs throughout the upper occupational stratum, it is most visible within the petite bourgeoisie. Cubans are regarded as competitors against local capitalists in the few areas that have not been taken over by United States firms. Carr puts it as follows:

> unable to beat [the large American corporations], the Puerto Rican business community had no alternative but to join them and become their servants or attempt to follow their example. . . . The one field open to local capitalists was real estate speculation and construction: hence the animus against the Cuban exile community, which was in direct competition in these fields. (1984, 263)

Third, and perhaps most important, Cuban exiles are regarded as staunch supporters of the United States and the pro-statehood cause. Carr asserts: "Cuban exiles are the new 100-percent Americans. . . . Scarcely surprising, the Cuban exiles vote for the party that is resolutely hostile to Cuba. . . . Their twenty thousand–odd votes are critical to the PNP [Partido Nuevo Progresista]" (1984, 263–64).

Survey data, reported in table 4.15, support the view that Cubans tend to favor the PNP: 67.2 percent of the respondents indicated such a preference.[3] However, it is impossible to determine whether the majority of Cubans would support statehood in a formal plebiscite on the status of Puerto Rico.

The political orientation of Cuban exiles has provoked the most vociferous complaints from proindependence Puerto Ricans. Marqués called the exiles "unconditional supporters of the United States . . . cynically colonialist . . . fierce enemies of Puerto Rico's national sovereignty and dignity" (1977, 208). Maldonado Denis has referred to Cuban exiles as "promoters of the blindest, most obscurantist anticommunism and antiindependence sentiment that the island has seen in a long time. . . . The century-old struggle of our people for independence does not mean anything to them, and they do not hesitate to praise and build up everything that is contrary to our desires for liberty" (1972, 182). In a stronger vein, a Marxist-nationalist group threatened that "the day will come when [Cubans] will be tried as traitors to the fatherland" (cited in Carr 1984, 264).

Other Puerto Ricans, however, have reacted positively to Cuban exiles. As stated earlier, Muñoz Marín encouraged Cuban exile professionals to immigrate to Puerto Rico. In the early 1960s the then rector of the University of Puerto Rico, Jaime Benítez, actively recruited Cuban intellectuals (Delgado Imbert 1989). While the Cubans' "100 percent Americanism" may have alienated some Puerto Ricans, proponents of statehood admire this trait in the exiles. Even a partisan of independence, the writer José Luis González, has asserted that Cuban exiles have set an example for Puerto Ricans in their struggle to preserve their national identity:

> Cuban immigrants, counterrevolutionaries in their country of origin and supporters for the most part of the Puerto Rican political right, have contributed something to the local society that transcends their conservative political attitudes. . . . No matter how counterrevolutionary and admirer of the United States a Cuban may be, he will never harbor any doubts about his national identity (which is quite different from his legal citizenship). (1986, 30)

Conclusion

The socioeconomic profile of Cuban exiles in Puerto Rico fits the middleman group pattern. Cubans' educational attainment and median income surpass those of Puerto Ricans. Cubans in Puerto Rico concentrate in prestigious and well-remunerated occupations. Many Cubans work for themselves; in the Cobas sample almost half of these are traders. Cubans who work for others tend to be employed in Cuban or non–Puerto Rican firms. Additionally, Cuban entrepreneurs rely on the in-group. The vast majority of Cuban business partnerships involve coethnics. Cuban employees hold positions of trust in coethnic businesses. Like other middleman groups, Cubans have aroused antagonism from the receiving society. They are charged with middleman group foibles: a feeling of superiority, unbridled ambition, and political disloyalty. Like other middleman groups, Cubans have allies who admire their industriousness and partisanship to the cause of statehood.

But unlike middleman groups, Cubans are not completely encapsulated. The extent of their relationships with the local society, including marriage, is notable. These relationships, however, tend to concentrate within the middle and upper strata of Puerto Rican society. This pattern is not without precedent among middleman groups. Germans in Imperial Russia behaved similarly (Armstrong 1976). A small change in religious affiliation, from the Lutheran to the Orthodox Church, was all that was required for the incorporation of Germans to the upper stratum of Russian society. For the majority of Cubans, who are Roman Catholics, incorporation to Puerto Rican society does not even require a change in religious affiliation.

Two additional important factors work against Cubans' remaining long in the middleman role. First, Cubans do not constitute a minority group in the sense that they do not experience serious discrimination and persecution. This does not mean that Cubans do not face antagonism and social exclusion. But in comparison to other middleman groups, such as Jews and Koreans, hostility toward Cubans in Puerto Rico is minor. Second, as Armstrong (1976) has pointed out, the existence of a homeland to which a middleman group may eventually return lessens the likelihood that it will remain permanently in the middleman role. Cubans have a homeland to which they may return, if circumstances permit, and this provides them with the option to leave the middleman position. Unless a new influx of Cuban immigrants arrives, Cubans are likely to disappear as a middleman group in the coming years.

But that Cubans seem to constitute a transitory middleman group does not mean that they have already lost their group identity. As will be shown in the following chapters, Cubans still maintain a strong sense of national identity. In the next chapter we will analyze the impact of economic specialization among Cubans on their attachment to the in-group.

5

Consequences of Participation in the Ethnic Economy

Simmel (1964) and Bonacich and Modell (1980) posit links between clannishness and a sense of estrangement and participation in the ethnic economy. The purpose of this chapter is to conduct an empirical test of these propositions using data from the Cobas survey.

Participation in the Ethnic Economy, Clannishness, and Estrangement

While writers such as Shils (1975) see ethnic attachment as a primordial connection, Cohen (1969), Leon (1970), Patterson (1975), Scott (1990), and others assert that such attachment is tied to practical needs. Rather than being a fundamental link, they argue, ethnicity is a bond that is invoked as needs dictate. As Wallman puts it, ethnicity "can be regarded as a resource which will, for some purposes and in some situations, be mobilized to the advantage of a social, cultural or racial category of people" (1979, ix). This conception is incorporated into a formal proposition by Bonacich and Modell (1980), who state that participants in the ethnic economy are more attached to the in-group than are other coethnics. To put it differently, clannishness is displayed more strongly among group members who work for themselves or a coethnic than among those who work in the wider economy.

As Bonacich and Modell see it, there are several reasons for such an attachment. First, members of the ethnic economy are "separated from those outside the group except when the latter are clients, a relationship that does not foster close ties" (1980, 22). Second, in-group allegiance offers practical payoffs. Ethnic economy employees get access to jobs, learn business lines, and eventually may obtain help from their employers to start their own businesses. Entrepreneurs may rely on coethnics for financial help, credit, or business tips. Since all of this is done in the name of ethnicity, ethnic economy members derive practical benefits from their good standing in the group, and a good way to enhance one's standing in the group is to be a loyal ethnic.

In sum, material concerns provide a strong impetus for in-group loyalty. To be sure, such concerns are not the only force behind the attachment of ethnic economy members to the in-group. However, as Bonacich and Modell see it (1980, 22), material considerations exert a crucial influence.

The estrangement hypothesis derives from the work of Simmel (1964, 403), who sees the stranger as the trader and the trader as stranger. One reason for the link between ethnic economy specialization and stranger status is the animus of the host society toward participants in the ethnic economy (Bonacich 1973). Faced with this animosity, ethnic economy members react by staying attached to the homeland, assuming they could return there if desired, and do not set roots in the host society. Additionally, ethnic economy participation produces estrangement from the receiving society because middleman traders avoid close ties with their host society customers; such ties interfere with business. When traders are strangers to their clients, they can conduct business in an objective manner and extend credit only to those who are able to pay (Foster 1974; Geertz 1963).

Testing the Assumption of Utilitarian Reasons

Although Bonacich and Modell (1984, 22) emphasize the utilitarian basis of in-group attachment, they recognize that another reason for the more intense clannishness of ethnic economy members is their separation from other groups. The coexistence of these two sources of in-group attachment gives rise to an ambiguity. The typical middleman group, such as Koreans in Los Angeles and Pakistanis in Manchester, stands out from the host society because of language, race, or religion. The isolation of group members in an ethnic economy tends to maintain their cultural differences. Under these conditions, it is difficult to assess whether ethnic economy members stick to the in-group because of utilitarian reasons or because they are unfamiliar with the ways of the receiving society. By the same token, it is also hard to tell whether ethnic economy members remain estranged from the receiving society because traders find it useful to remain aloof or because their encapsulation makes them, first, unable to learn the ways of the out-group and, second, look peculiar to their hosts, who reject them.

Since differences with regard to culture and language between Cubans and Puerto Ricans are minimal,[1] the clannishness of ethnic economy members could not be attributed to an inability to interact with out-group members and a lack of familiarity with the ways of the host society. In fact, a higher display of clannishness on the part of ethnic economy members would support Bonacich and Modell's and Simmel's assumption of utilitarian motivation. For this reason, the sample of Cuban exiles from San Juan is eminently suitable to test the assumption in the propositions advanced by Simmel and Bonacich and Modell.

Class Distinctions in the Ethnic Economy

Since informality colors the relationships between owners and employees in the ethnic economy, class distinctions there tend to be less clearly defined than in the wider society (Waldinger 1984). However, socioeconomic differences persist even within the ethnic economy. The argument is made here that employees confront distinctive circumstances that make them more likely than owners to adhere to Simmel's and Bonacich and Modell's predictions. Stated differently, when owners and employees in the ethnic economy are compared with coethnics that work in the general economy regarding in-group attachment and estrangement, we expect that ethnic economy employees will stand out more than owners.

This expectation has several bases. First, ethnic business employees are less financially secure than owners. In times of crisis they have a greater need to turn to the in-group for relief. Second, employees depend on owners' goodwill to have jobs and to secure assistance to start businesses of their own. Thus, employees are particularly dependent on the in-group. Owners, on the other hand, experience a greater need to maintain regular contacts outside the ethnic community. They deal with bankers, sales representatives, and suppliers. This need to relate to outsiders produces more opportunities to establish friendships and other ties outside the ethnic community.

Table 5.1. Description of dependent variables used in regression analyses

Variable Names	Description	Range
Cuban friends	Percent of respondent's friends who are Cuban	0–0 percent — 100–100 percent
Cuban partner	If respondent were looking for a business partner, how important would it be for partner to be Cuban	1: Very little — 4: A lot
Cuban spouse	If respondent (or son) were looking for a woman to marry, how important would it be for the woman to be Cuban	1: Very little — 4: A lot
Organizations	Respondent belongs to at least one Cuban organization in Puerto Rico	0: No — 1: Yes
Stranger	How strange respondent feels in Puerto Rico	1: Perfectly at home — 3: Very little or not at all[a]
Citizen	Is respondent U.S. citizen	0: No 1: Yes

[a]These two categories were combined due to a sparseness of respondents in highest category.

Concerning estrangement from the receiving society, employees have fewer incentives to set roots in the place of their migration. First, being proprietors, owners have a higher economic stake in the receiving society. Second, owners are less free to migrate than employees, since owners must sell their property before moving and this can be a slow task. Third, while employees would receive some gains from obtaining local citizenship, such as being eligible to vote in elections, owners would gain the additional advantage of a more secure status for their property. Fourth, because they enjoy a higher economic situation, owners are in a better position to afford the naturalization process. Fifth, because of their more secure economic situation, owners feel less vulnerable to the antagonism of the host society and consequently are less estranged from that society. Thus, while owners can use their economic position and contacts in the host society to protect themselves against antagonism, employees' access to such resources is more limited. To summarize, we expect that ethnic economy employees will stand out more than owners regarding in-group attachment and estrangement when contrasted with coethnics in the wider economy.

Method

The six dependent variables used in the analyses are described in table 5.1. Cuban friends, Cuban partner, Cuban spouse, and Organizations tap attachment to the in-group. Stranger and Citizen measure estrangement from the receiving society.

A regression model was fitted for each dependent variable. Each model contained seven independent variables representing the respondents' characteristics as follows: 1) age, 2) length of residence in Puerto Rico, 3) education in years, 4) yearly income, 5) prestige of current occupation (coded according to Treiman's (1977) scale), 6) Cuban employee (a dichotomous variable coded 1 if respondent was an employee in a Cuban business, 0 if otherwise), and 7) Owner (a dichotomous variable coded 1 if respondent was self-employed, 0 if otherwise). The first five independent variables are needed as statistical controls since they are probably associated with ethnic economy participation and the dependent variables (see Cobas 1985, 439, n. 4).

The main purpose of the models is to assess whether, after controlling for relevant variables, employees in Cuban firms (represented by the variable "Cuban Employee") and self-employed individuals ("Owner") differ significantly from respondents employed in the general economy. Stated differently, we will determine whether Cuban Employee and Owner have statistically significant effects on the dependent variables after adjusting for the other five independent variables.[2]

Table 5.2. Results of ordinary least squares regression: dependent variable "Cuban Friends" (proportion of close friends who are Cuban)

Predictor	Coefficient estimate	Standard error	t	p<
Age	.06	.21	.29	.77
Residence	-.93	.49	-1.90	.06
Education	1.90	1.98	.96	.34
Income[a]	.05	.02	2.00	.05
Occupational prestige	-.09	.25	-.36	.72
Cuban employee	20.18	6.93	2.91	.00
Owner	22.01	5.46	4.03	.00

Note: N = 212; eight cases missing.
[a]To avoid a large number of leading zeros, the coefficient estimate and standard error for this variable are multiplied by 100.

Results

Results of the statistical analysis pertaining to the dependent variables measuring attachment to the in-group appear in tables 5.2 through 5.5.[3] Although both Cuban employee and Owner have significant effects on an indicator of clannishness, Cuban friends, their effects on the remaining dependent variables are not significant. Thus, neither Cuban business employees nor owners are more likely than other coethnics to prefer a Cuban for a business partner or a marriage partner or to belong to Cuban organizations. It is important to note that age is a more consistent predictor of clannishness than is ethnic economy participation. Tables 5.3 and 5.5 show that age has significant effects on preference for a Cuban partner and membership in Cuban organizations.

Results concerning estrangement appear in tables 5.6 and 5.7. Observe that employees in Cuban businesses are much less likely than coethnics working in the general economy to have become U.S. citizens. Additionally, their greater sense of estrangement barely fails to meet the criterion of statistical significance. Owners, however, are not less prone to have become U.S. citizens and do not show a higher sense of estrangement when compared with coethnics outside the ethnic economy.

In summary, the self-employed and employees in Cuban businesses show a modestly higher degree of attachment to the in-group than do coethnics working in the general economy. Additionally, Cuban business employees are less likely to have become U.S. citizens than coethnics employed in the general economy. The self-employed, however, did not display such a propensity.

Conclusion

Results provided weak support for the Bonacich-Modell hypothesis. Owners and employees of Cuban businesses stood out from other coethnics only with regard to the percentage of their friends who were Cuban. Otherwise, ethnic economy members were not significantly more clannish than other coethnics.

As concerns Simmel's hypothesis, Cuban business employees show a greater sense of estrangement than do other coethnics. Some of the reasons for the greater estrangement of employees were discussed above. Employees have less stake in Puerto Rico than do owners. Employees have fewer resources to isolate themselves from the wider society and as a result are more likely to experience friction than owners.

Table 5.3. Results of multinomial logistic regression: dependent variable: "Cuban partner" (how important would it be for a business partner to be Cuban)

Predictor	Chi square	p<
Age	9.98	.02
Residence	9.76	.02
Education	5.29	.15
Income	2.23	.53
Occupational prestige	1.92	.59
Cuban employee	1.50	.68
Owner	1.76	.62

Note: N = 210; ten cases missing.

Table 5.4. Results of multinomial logistic regression: dependent variable "Cuban spouse" (how important would it be for a son to marry a Cuban)

Predictor	Chi square	p<
Age	1.61	.66
Residence	6.33	.10
Education	5.87	.12
Income	2.04	.56
Occupational prestige	.50	.92
Cuban employee	3.07	.38
Owner	.97	.81

Note: N = 207; thirteen cases missing.

Table 5.5. Results of binary logistic regression: dependent variable "Organizations" (respondent belongs to at least one Cuban exile organization)

Predictor	Coefficient estimate	Standard error	Chi square	p<
Age	.03	.02	4.75	.03
Residence	-.03	.03	.90	.34
Education	.20	.14	1.86	.17
Income[a]	.03	.02	2.58	.11
Occupational prestige[b]	-.03	.18	.03	.86
Cuban employee	-.22	.52	.18	.67
Owner	.33	.39	.72	.40

Note: N = 213; seven cases missing.

[a]To avoid leading zeros, the coefficient estimate and standard error for this variable are multiplied by 1,000.

[b]To avoid leading zeros, the coefficient estimate and standard error for this variable are multiplied by 10.

Table 5.6. Results of multinomial logistic regression: dependent variable "Stranger" (how strange respondent feels in Puerto Rico)

Predictor	Chi square	p<
Age	1.81	.40
Residence	5.09	.08
Education	1.03	.60
Income	.41	.81
Occupational prestige	.53	.77
Cuban employee	5.53	.06
Self-employed	3.67	.16

Note: N = 212; eight cases missing.

Table 5.7. Results of binary logistic regression: dependent variable "Citizen" (respondent is U.S. citizen)

Predictor	Coefficient estimate	Standard error	Chi square	p<
Age	-.01	.02	.50	.48
Residence	.21	.05	19.28	.00
Education	.06	.19	.12	.73
Income[a]	.08	.03	8.12	.00
Occupational prestige	.05	.03	3.56	.06
Cuban employee	-1.49	.62	5.73	.02
Self-employed	-.55	.59	.86	.35

Note: N = 213; seven 7 cases missing.
[a]To avoid leading zeros, the coefficient estimate and standard error for this variable are multiplied by 1,000.

The data indicated that knowing a respondent's age was more useful in predicting his clannishness than knowing whether or not he was an ethnic economy participant. That is, older respondents, regardless of whether they were participants in the ethnic economy, were more attached to the in-group than younger respondents. This fact suggests that symbolic displays of attachment to the Cuban community reflect the patriotism and loyalty of those who lived longer in the homeland more than the self-interest of ethnic economy participants. We will return to the topic of generational differences among Cuban exiles in later chapters.

In chapter 4 we showed that Cuban entrepreneurs chose partners disproportionately from the in-group and placed coethnic employees in positions of trust. And in chapters that follow, we will discuss several manifestations of in-group attachment among Cubans in Puerto Rico, beginning with the most active Cuban voluntary association in San Juan. In light of these clear instances of in-group predilection, why is there not an open proclamation of an exclusivist ideology? Because businesses are visible and Cubans have enemies, ethnic economy members are careful. In particular, they want to avoid living up to their reputation of being foreign and disloyal to Puerto Rico. As a result, they play down their characteristics that their enemies may use against them, such as a sense of "cultural superiority," or clannishness.

6

La Casa Cuba

An Immigrant Community in San Juan

In contrast to other Latin American societies (Butterworth and Chance 1981, 136), voluntary associations played an important role in prerevolutionary Cuba. Social clubs, mutual aid societies, professional associations, sports and recreational organizations, and religious sodalities proliferated among all sectors of Cuban society and continue to flourish in exile.[1] Before 1959 Havana had numerous Spanish associations such as the Centro Gallego, the Centro Asturiano, and the Casino Español; Chinese associations such as the Centro Chino; and Afro-Cuban organizations such as the Club Atenas. In addition, Havana had other popular associations such as the Club Naútico; professional associations of lawyers, physicians, and teachers; and exclusive yacht, tennis, and country clubs of the white elite.[2]

Voluntary associations in Cuba fulfilled such functions as medical care, entertainment, social advancement, adjustment to urban life, group solidarity, and cultural survival. They did not disappear suddenly with the postrevolutionary exodus; on the contrary, the exiles transplanted a long-standing web of Cuban civic and political organizations to the United States and Puerto Rico, often under the same names and with the same purposes. To illustrate, Miami alone has 114 *municipios en el exilio,* regional associations comprising former residents of different municipalities (Boswell and Curtis 1984, 176). Some of these municipios also function in Puerto Rico but are not as active as in the United States.[3]

The Círculo Cubano de Puerto Rico, or Casa Cuba, as it is commonly known, is the most active exile group in San Juan.[4] According to its leaders, in the 1980s Casa Cuba had a membership of one thousand families—or six thousand individual members, almost one-third of all San Juan Cubans.[5] According to its former president Manuel González, Casa Cuba is the largest Cuban club outside Cuba (*San Juan Star*, September 4, 1984).

In contrast to most Cuban organizations in exile, Casa Cuba existed prior to the 1959 revolution. When it was founded, the number of Cubans in Puerto Rico was small. But the club grew rapidly during the 1960s as a result of increased migration from Cuba. In this chapter we will analyze the changes experienced by Casa Cuba since Cubans began to play the role of middleman group in Puerto Rico. We will examine Casa Cuba as an example of typical middleman group behavior: encapsulation within the in-group. Above all, we will attempt to answer the following question: Why has Casa Cuba survived for more than forty years? Our goal is to unearth the meaning of ethnic identity among members of this Cuban club in San Juan.

Origins

On February 24, 1949, forty-five Cuban émigrés in San Juan formed the Círculo Cubano de Puerto Rico to "attain the spiritual unity and to foster the fraternal relations between all Cubans residing in Puerto Rico and the friends of Cuba who may deserve that distinction" (Círculo Cubano 1980, 17). The founding members of the club included the Cuban consul in Puerto Rico, the manager of the Bacardí Rum Corporation, and the prosperous entrepreneur Antonio Ferré Bacallao, whose son would later become governor of Puerto Rico. The club's initial activities—dances, raffles, fairs, and dinners—were geared to raise funds for a clubhouse. An official bulletin was published irregularly, and meetings were held at a Cuban restaurant. Club members donated blood, celebrated patriotic dates, sponsored Carnival dances, and performed charity work. They also established personal connections with prominent local figures, such as Governor Muñoz Marín, and with elite local institutions, such as the Caparra Country Club. In 1956 a clubhouse was inaugurated at a cost of over $100 thousand.

The club originated in a closely knit group with plenty of resources and social contacts. Its activities reflected the tastes of a leisure class that enjoyed drinking, playing dominoes and cards, and swimming in the ocean.

In 1956 the club had only 152 members; most of them knew each other well, and the whole organization had a small-scale character, almost like an extended family (Círculo Cubano 1980, 18–28). In 1949 membership dues were two dollars every three months, but dues were raised in 1959 to five dollars and again in 1961 to seven dollars. In those days that was a substantial amount of money to pay for membership in a social organization.

A Decade of Change

Most of the founders of the Círculo Cubano were not political exiles: they lived in Puerto Rico for personal and professional reasons. Before 1959 the club had more Puerto Rican than Cuban members. But with the massive influx of anti-Castro exiles, the club took on a new life. In 1963 the club had only sixty members, and the admission fee was reduced from one hundred to fifty dollars to facilitate the admission of the new immigrants. In 1965 the Círculo Cubano merged with the Lyceum Cubano, an exile organization. Although this union would ensure the institution's viability, it led many of the old members of the Círculo Cubano to leave the club. A clear conflict of interests divided the early immigrants from the recent political refugees. By the end of the 1960s the vast majority of members were exiles from the Cuban revolution. The outlook of this new generation was embodied in Jorge Quadreny, president of the club between 1967 and 1974, who expanded the club's facilities to accommodate a booming membership. During this time the club lost both its extended family character and its apolitical perspective.

The 1960s witnessed extraordinary physical growth and social effervescence in Casa Cuba. In 1969 the club had its first crew team, an event of particular importance because Cuban exiles had introduced this sport to Puerto Rico. In 1971 the club inaugurated the island's first squash court, which instantly became a landmark of Cuban enterprise and prosperity. Carnivals, debutante balls, and beauty pageants were added to an already crowded yearly cycle of festivities. The first issue of the magazine *Casa de Cuba*, devoted to covering the intense social life of the club's members, saw light. The club purchased neighboring land for a second parking lot, added a second story to the main building, and became an important center of recreation for San Juan's Cuban community.

Growth and Influx

During the 1970s the club's tendency to grow in all directions—sideways, upward, to the front, and even inside—continued. The only barrier to expansion seemed to be the ocean to the north. High-rise condominiums such as Comodoro and Varadero (both names come from Cuba) were built almost as appendixes to the club, because many of its occupants were Casa Cuba members. The ceremonies to crown the club's queen became, according to the club's magazine, "more and more splendorous," and in 1978 the Carnivals were presented to the general public for the first time at the Roberto Clemente Sports Coliseum in San Juan. Casa Cuba members also ventured outside the club's frontiers in other areas: they organized national and international athletic tournaments, promoted Cuban music and dance, deepened their links with government authorities, and spread themselves to the surrounding area of Isla Verde. Cubans had created a distinct immigrant community in San Juan.

In the 1970s the Cuban exile community of Puerto Rico was still in a state of flux, which affected Casa Cuba. While numerous families came to San Juan, even larger numbers left for Miami. Between 1970 and 1980 the Cuban population of Puerto Rico decreased from 26,000 to 22,811 individuals (U.S. Department of Commerce 1984a, table 43). Many club members, including past presidents and officers, relocated outside Puerto Rico. At the same time, new families joined Círculo Cubano. This coming and going of people gave Casa Cuba a transient character: many of its members were not certain to stay or settle permanent roots in Puerto Rico. Farewell and welcome parties became increasingly common, serving as reminders that exiles really belong neither here nor there. As mentioned earlier, some scholars (Bonacich 1973) identify this ambivalence toward the receiving society as a typical middleman group trait.

Consolidation and Renovation

By 1984 Casa Cuba's membership was one hundred times larger than when the club was founded. Its rustic original club building was replaced by a larger modern one. Its land value was much higher than its original price. Members paid a forty-dollar monthly quota, plus a onetime two-hundred-dollar entrance fee. Yet the basic purpose of the institution did not change substantially. The 1979 *Reglamento* states that the Círculo's main objective is "to promote the rapprochement, mutual understanding, and friendship among all democratic Cubans who live outside their fatherland and especially between Cubans and Puerto Ricans" (page 3). In 1949 Casa Cuba sought to "promulgate Cuban culture throughout the island [of Puerto Rico]"; by 1979 the emphasis was on "keeping the image of the distant Fatherland alive at all times and make it known to the new generations." The current constitution is more nationalistic and militant in tone than its earlier version: a clause clearly asserts that the club supports "the reconquest of the fatherland enslaved by international communism" (Círculo Cubano 1979, 4).

Today the club retains its initial upper- and middle-class orientation; most of its members belong to the upper levels of management, commerce, and the professions. The list of routine activities is similar to that of the 1950s: dances, parties, games, time at the beach, enjoying the company of friends and relatives. The preservation of Cuban customs and values continues to be the club's main purpose. The main difference between the Casa Cuba of the 1990s and that of 1959 is the experience of a revolution and the trauma of exile. Political ideology became the principal axis of ethnic identity for Cubans in San Juan.

Casa Cuba's Future

Casa Cuba's president in the mid 1980s was Manuel González, an energetic and articulate Cuban businessman in his early forties. During an interview held in June 1984 he discussed his goals: "We want Casa Cuba to be the center of Cuban cultural life in Puerto Rico. . . . If Casa Cuba ceases to exist, Cubans will disappear as an ethnic group." For González and other leaders renovation and improvement of the physical facilities, the dominant preoccupation of earlier club officials, was less salient than the organization's mission. In 1984 Casa Cuba had become a mature institution with a smaller but more stable membership than in the past. As González saw it, the challenge was to make the club the main gathering place for Cubans in Puerto Rico. Thus, several regional associations—among them *orientales* (from Oriente province), *guantanameros* (from the city of Guantánamo), and *villaclareños* (from the Las Villas province)—held their activities at Casa Cuba. Such activities typically included masses, fairs, raffles, dances, and dinners.

One of the club's most pressing problems today is attracting Cuban youth. A vice president of Casa Cuba in the 1980s, Mario Campos, stated in a newspaper interview that "our main interest right now is our young people"

(*San Juan Star,* September 4, 1984). The younger generation of Cuban exiles do not seem interested in the club's affairs after they reach adulthood. According to González, "The club should exist so that the younger ones may love their country—which is Puerto Rico—as well as ours, Cuba." Many activities, such as judo, basketball, and ballet, are geared toward this age group. This trend led one reporter to conclude that Cubans in Puerto Rico are concerned "not so much, perhaps, about the fate of Fidel Castro in the land they left behind as about the fate of their children in their adopted land" (*San Juan Star,* September 4, 1984). Cuban exiles realize that the future of any ethnic group is in the hands of the second and subsequent generations.

In sum, Casa Cuba saw extraordinary growth in the last four decades. The club's assets, for instance, increased elevenfold between 1969 and 1977 (*Casa de Cuba,* May 1978). The history of this association reflects the socioeconomic evolution of the Cuban community in Puerto Rico—from a small group of interconnected families to a middleman group. At the outset the club consisted of a tiny nucleus of immigrants who wanted to stay in touch. It later became a larger community of exiles, whose goals include the promotion of anticommunist ideology, free enterprise, and ethnic identity. In this manner the association has been a viable institution for several cohorts of Cubans in Puerto Rico.

Social Composition of the Club

The membership of Casa Cuba consists primarily of middle-class Cuban families. From 1971 to 1978 the periodical *Casa de Cuba* published a professional directory that included more than eighteen specialized occupations, ranging from physician and psychologist to fashion model and sales representative. They were all white-collar jobs, principally professional, technical, and business occupations. According to a piece published in 1974, the typical jobs of club members were in office work, the professions, business, and manufacturing. Many of the members were housewives and students. Duany's survey showed that college-educated white-collar workers predominated in Casa Cuba's membership. From this occupational profile one can surmise middle and high levels of income and education. Another social status indicator, more informal in nature, is the members' cars: the club's parking lot is always crowded with expensive models.

The members' lifestyle is lavishly illustrated in the social section of *Casa de Cuba,* which chronicles events such as weddings, christenings, birthday celebrations, and graduations. The style of these reports is formulaic and flowery. Women are typically described as "distinguished and kind" ladies; young women are "beautiful and elegant *señoritas.*" Men, on the other hand, are usually referred to as "our dear associate Mr. So-and-So." These accounts pay close attention to family names and genealogy. Not only do the members of Casa Cuba come from the upper crust of society, they are also related among each other by kinship and marriage ties. The question that arises, then, is how this large interconnected group is organized.

Formal Organization

The rules of 1979 define three statuses within the club: members, guests, and officers. Each member and officer is required to show proper identification before entering the club and to pay a special fee if bringing a guest. These rules are clearly designed to keep the club closed to intruders.

The rules also specify the ideal member behavior. Among other things, members are not to "utter obscene words nor raise their voices unduly, nor to make offensive or denigrating gestures, nor in any way disturb the order and peace of the social club, nor in any way cause other members to be indignant, disgusted, or distressed" (Círculo Cubano 1979, 18). Placing bets, conducting business, and political activity are forbidden. Members may be reprimanded, suspended, or expelled if they behave disrespectfully toward other members, physically or verbally attack them, or vandalize or appropriate club property. Proper behavior also requires cooperation with club officers, formal distance between elders and minors, considerate conduct toward others, and control of irrational impulses. Thus the rules attempt to define the basis of sociability; sanction values such as respectfulness, decorum, and courtesy; and delineate good taste for members.

Admission Procedures

How does one become a member of Círculo Cubano? The basic mechanism is member sponsorship: "Any person aspiring to enter the Association must include on his/her application the signed endorsement of two active members" (Círculo Cubano 1979, 16). Applications must be posted on the club's bulletin board for public inspection, and any member who has objections to the applicant must so inform the board of directors. Final approval is in the hands of this board, and voting is secret. If accepted, a new member pays a onetime entrance fee and a monthly quota. Failure to make payment for three consecutive months may result in expulsion from the association.

These practices originated in private clubs in prerevolutionary Cuba. For example, the Havana Country Club employed a similar admission process based on sponsors and secret votes. This method of applicant selection ensures that only individuals who know club members and survive public examination will be admitted. The club reserves the right of admission and, according to the rules, is not obligated "in any case to notify failure to accept a candidate for membership, or to explain the reasons it had for rejection" (Círculo Cubano 1979, 16).

The Government of an Exile Community

The rules describe in detail the club's ruling body; more than half of its pages are devoted to this topic. Casa Cuba has a presidential government in the tradition of many Latin American republics, including Cuba. The president can break ties, represent the association at all official acts, take emergency measures when required, and direct all committees and activities sponsored by the board of directors. Next in importance are the secretary, who is in charge of bureaucratic and clerical matters, and the treasurer, who administers the club's funds. The remaining fifteen members of the ruling body, called *directivos,* are assigned particular tasks such as public relations, social activities, civic and patriotic events, and sports and recreation. Officers are elected every two years by direct vote of all members over eighteen years of age, including women (since 1978). The political structure of the club thus follows the democratic principles so ardently espoused by Cuban exiles.

Formal Structure versus Everyday Behavior

As is true in all voluntary associations, a discrepancy exists between the expected and actual behavior of Casa Cuba's members. Although the rules specify that no one will be excluded from membership on the basis of nationality, the vast majority of members are Cuban, plus a few of their Puerto Rican friends. This is an association based on national origin and, to a great extent, on ethnic exclusiveness. Though in theory the club is open to anyone, in practice it represents a closed society. Most of its activities do not attract individuals outside the Cuban community.

Real life contradicts written rules in other respects. The club would have to have its own police force to enforce prohibitions against screaming foul language, games of chance, business transactions, and political activity. It seems unlikely that Cuban exiles will refrain from distributing anti-Castro literature, selling their products, or placing bets when they are in the club.

Politics and Public Image

In the 1980s Casa Cuba became the object of a controversy that sheds light on the discrepancy between official norms and actual behavior. A week after the 1984 elections, Severo Colberg, then Speaker of the Puerto Rican House of Representatives and member of the Partido Popular Demócrata, which supports commonwealth status for Puerto Rico, accused the club of being "pro-Batista and anti-Puerto Rican" (*El Reportero,* November 10, 1984). Colberg added that Casa Cuba had collaborated closely with the pro-statehood party (PNP). The club's president immediately responded that "Casa Cuba has never participated in Puerto Rico's electoral process, nor has it supported any candidate or party whatsoever" (*El Reportero,* November 17, 1984). The debate touched upon not only the political affiliations of Casa Cuba's members but also their emotional attachment to Puerto Rico.[6]

As on other occasions, this incident revealed that public discussion on Cubans in Puerto Rico invariably brings up the issue of how the foreigners feel about the receiving country. In Colberg's opinion, Cubans despise Puerto Ricans; a Cuban exile retorted that "Casa Cuba is integrated by numerous Cuban and Puerto Rican families of diverse ideologies" (*El Reportero,* December 3, 1984).

Colberg's views resonate with a common stereotype concerning Cubans in Puerto Rico: that they are unconditionally in favor of statehood and the PNP. Many Puerto Ricans undoubtedly perceive Casa Cuba as a bastion of pro-American and pro-statehood ideology.[7] Members of Casa Cuba correctly point out that their club has never taken an official public position on the political status of Puerto Rico. However, Gov. Carlos Romero Barceló, leader of the PNP, was welcomed by an enthusiastic full house during the summer of 1981. More recently PNP governor Pedro Roselló visited the club. Many of the exiles are closely identified with the PNP—the party founded in 1968 by Luis Ferré, a Puerto Rican industrialist whose father was a Cuban émigré and a founder of the Círculo Cubano.

A Carnival of Exile

An account of a major cultural event—Carnival night at Casa Cuba—may throw more light on the exiles' behavior. The *comparsas de carnaval* (the word *comparsa* refers to a group of masked dancers) are part of Cuba's rich musical heritage, reenacted in Puerto Rico by members of the Círculo Cubano. Held every year before Lent, Carnival generates as much excitement as the other three most popular rituals on the club's calendar: *quinceañeras* (debutante balls), *coronaciones* (crowning of the club's queen), and election of club officers. For the exiles Carnival represents a mechanism to preserve the cultural traditions of their homeland in a foreign land. Presently we will analyze Carnival as an important clue to the exiles' worldview. Although we will focus on Carnival night in 1984, more-recent observations confirm that the celebration did not change much in the 1990s.

In the 1980s the comparsas at the club consisted mostly of second-generation immigrants, particularly girls under the age of sixteen. Most participants were young people who frequented the same social circles and knew each other well. A good portion of the audience comprised middle-aged individuals related to the participants by kinship and friendship ties. Carnival is primarily a ritual event put on by the second generation in order to maintain the traditions of the first generation of Cubans in Puerto Rico.

In 1984 Carnival night interrupted the club's normal activities for an entire weekend. A large wooden structure, built on top of the basketball and squash courts, became a temporary stage. In addition to the permanent bar and restaurant, small drink and food stands were set up for the occasion. Members stopped playing basketball, squash, dominoes, and canasta to attend the event, though a few seemed oblivious to it and preferred to watch television in a corner of the main hall. Most people, however, were excited by the bright lights, colorful costumes, well-rehearsed dances, and lively music of Cuba.

Each comparsa had from 20 to 30 members; all told, about 120 to 150 persons participated directly in the dancing. There were far more females than males: the ratio was about three to one. Most of the males were boys under age six, but among those over thirty, men and women were almost equally represented. Two of the five comparsas consisted of children, another two of adolescents, and the last one of young adults. Most participants and members of the audience were white.

"Cubans First, Puerto Ricans Second"

The 1984 Carnival started with the presentation and promenade of the club's queen and guests of honor. Then the marshals for that year's Carnival were introduced, a married couple of television actors from Cuba who resided in Puerto Rico. Ofelia D'Acosta gave thanks for the honor and claimed that although Puerto Rico was her new fatherland, she was proud to be Cuban. Her husband, Tino Acosta, went further when he stated that they were "Cubans first, Puerto Ricans second, but above all Americans." His words were received with a standing ovation. Then the queen and her guests stepped down from the stage and the comparsas started, beginning with the youngest one.

All performers wore elaborate costumes, and girls as well as women were heavily made up. They performed choreographed dances to Cuban music of the 1950s, popular when many of them had not even been born. The last comparsa dramatized the mythical fatherland before the revolution: *la Cuba del ayer,* yesterday's Cuba. The master of ceremonies introduced this comparsa with the words "Cuba is our past, Puerto Rico our present, and Cuba our future." Although the first comparsas danced to music from Cuba and other countries, the last one relied exclusively on Cuban songs. The comparsa featured popular social types of prerevolutionary Cuba: the *tamalero* (tamale vendor), the *manicero* (peanut vendor), the Spanish *bodeguero* (shopkeeper), the Chinese *billetero* (lottery ticket vendor), and the voluptuous mulatto woman. It also conjured up the *solar,* the slum tenement house that so many exiles had heard of but never lived in. In brief, Carnival represents a nostalgic re-creation of Cuban culture by the middle-class white exiles.

A Sunday at Casa Cuba

Although Carnival is held only once a year, Casa Cuba routinely acquires a carnivalesque atmosphere, particularly on summer Sundays. The quantity and variety of activities are striking: squash, basketball, volleyball, dominoes, canasta, bingo, swimming, eating at the restaurant, talking, and much more. All of these activities take place contiguously and continuously within a reduced space, often overlapping with each other. Tennis balls frequently bounce into the basketball court, as do basketballs into the squash area. A man wearing shorts and a T-shirt may socialize with a well-dressed lady. From the most casual to the most formal, any kind of fashion may be seen on a given afternoon. Casa Cuba's ambiance is always festive, though an observer may not know that the exiles are celebrating.

Cubans reaffirm their ethnic identity through an elaborate ritual of integration and intensification. Every Sunday club members separate themselves physically and socially from the outside world. Once they enter the club, members extinguish their other social statuses: they are no longer managers or housewives, teachers or students, but Cubans among Cubans. On Mondays they return to their normal lives, strengthened by tokens of their nationality: the flag, the national anthem, the statues of the patriot José Martí and Our Lady of Charity, and, above all, their compatriots. This cycle of separation from the club community, transition, and reincorporation is repeated every week with slight variations. A Sunday at Casa Cuba symbolizes the constant passage between two social worlds: the interior world of the Cuban past and the exterior world of the Puerto Rican present.

Casa Cuba as a Network of Networks

We can now return to the question posed at the beginning of this chapter: Why does Casa Cuba continue to exist after more than forty years? Even today, the club serves as a base for its members to form and transform their interpersonal networks. The club's main function is to facilitate the individual management of one's relations with other members of the in-group. Casa Cuba maximizes the density and accessibility of social contacts within the immigrant community, thus reinforcing the typical encapsulation of middleman groups. Club members tend to raise their children, form their most lasting friendships, fall in love, and marry within the in-group; they sometimes even choose to live in the same vicinity, for example, in the predominantly Cuban condominiums near the club. Casa Cuba attempts to encompass all the stages of the life cycle—from birth to death—and all areas of the social life of its members. As Light points out, "clubs provide a private place to concoct business and political deals or to arrange marriages" (1984, 205).

The physical concentration of these interpersonal encounters among the exiles underlines how interconnected the Cuban community of San Juan is. A continuing exchange of goods and services takes place within the ethnic, class, and color boundaries of the club. A member may lend money to another, and the latter may provide business tips in return. Still another member may help a godchild to enter the university out of gratitude to the godchild's parents for help in finding his first job in Puerto Rico. These chains of reciprocity maintain the feelings of solidarity and cohesion among Cubans in Puerto Rico.

The club, then, represents an adaptation strategy aimed at coping with life in a foreign country. This strategy is characterized by a highly localized knot of personal linkages, the reliance on a closed system of social relations, and the development of multipurpose ethnic ties. The strategy's main goal is to establish a network of friends, ritual kin, and patrons that can help Cubans advance socially, economically, and politically. When such bonds carry over to the outside world, they provide a security system for the exiles. This encapsulation helps explain the Cubans' success in business and the professions, endeavors in which personal contacts can be useful in securing customers, credit, and other resources.

Conclusion

Through the years Casa Cuba has served several needs for its members: entertainment, cultural persistence, and social advancement. Like the Cuban clubs of Tampa at the beginning of the century, Casa Cuba meets "the practical needs of everyday life as well as the need for a moral sense of community" (Middleton 1981, 295). Founded by prerevolution émigrés, the club was overtaken by the more numerous and militant exiles of the 1960s. Its main purpose—to preserve and promote Cuban culture in Puerto Rico—remains intact, but its character evolved. In the beginning Casa Cuba gathered a small group of Cuban immigrants and a larger number of Puerto Rican families. At that time the club's main activities were geared toward offering opportunities for leisure and mingling to Cuban immigrants and their Puerto Rican friends. But in the 1960s the club became a reception center for newly arrived refugees from Cuba. In attracting large numbers of businessmen and professionals, Casa Cuba became an advocate of middleman group ideology.

Today Casa Cuba serves the interests of Cubans as a middleman group. First, it offers a place where its members, principally Cuban businessmen and professionals, may mingle with coethnics who share their social status. Second, Casa Cuba strengthens the bonds between Cubans in Puerto Rico and Cubans in the United States. We already mentioned that international contacts are a typical trait of middleman groups. Third, through linkages between Casa Cuba and elite Puerto Rican institutions, such as Caparra Country Club and Casa de España, members of the Cuban community can establish bonds with the Puerto Rican upper crust. As pointed out earlier, when no significant cultural or religious differences separate middleman groups from the receiving society, such groups tend to form alliances with, even intermarry, members of the local elite. In the following chapter we discuss other Cuban associations in Puerto Rico that fulfill similar functions.

7

Cuban Associations in Puerto Rico

Middleman groups tend to create many voluntary associations. These associations often strengthen in-group solidarity, bolster the group's reputation, maintain cultural traditions, and promote economic adaptation to the host society. One common strategy is to establish formal associations to reduce outside competition and channel the resources of the ethnic community (Waldinger et al. 1990). For instance, the Lebanese in prerevolutionary Cuba established nine different organizations, published a magazine, and broadcast a weekly radio program in both Arabic and Spanish (Safa 1960, 93). Similarly, the Chinese founded numerous trade, religious, and recreational associations in Guyana, Trinidad, and Jamaica (Fried 1958). Finally, Jewish Americans at the turn of the century developed a high degree of communal solidarity (Zenner 1991). In sum, voluntary associations foster the cultural identity and social solidarity of middleman groups as well as their business development.

This chapter presents a detailed study of the Unión de Cubanos en el Exilio, one of the most important Cuban organizations in Puerto Rico. In Duany's survey 7 percent of the respondents belonged to the Unión de Cubanos en el Exilio. In addition, we will provide an overview of other social, religious, and political exile organizations on the island. We will show that most of the Cuban associations in Puerto Rico express the exiles' collective behavior and ideology as a middleman group. Furthermore, we will interpret such voluntary associations as attempts to preserve the cultural identity of Cubans in exile. To be sure, some Cuban organizations in Puerto

Rico do not conform to petite bourgeois values and practices. But, as will be shown, they tend not to prosper.

The Unión de Cubanos en el Exilio: Charity and Mutual Aid

In the last chapter we analyzed Casa Cuba, Puerto Rico's main Cuban exile organization. We showed that as Cubans began to assume the middleman role in Puerto Rico, Casa Cuba changed from a club in which a small number of Cuban families socialized with their Puerto Rican friends to an association dedicated to the promotion of middleman group ideology. In this section we will show how the Unión de Cubanos en el Exilio (UCE) fulfills another important activity: improving the group's public image. Although UCE's explicit goal is to help members of the Cuban community, many of its activities are also intended to combat the reputation of Cubans in Puerto Rico as clannish and selfish merchants.

Although many of its members belong to Casa Cuba, UCE is a different type of voluntary association. According to Sara Fernández, one of the presidents of UCE during the 1980s, the association's purpose was quite clear. "We are not totally a social organization," she remarked during a personal interview. "Above all, we do charity work." Then she added: "There is no charity without vanity" (personal interview, June 6, 1984).

Although initially UCE was led by men and women, today it depends primarily on the efforts and resources of Cuban women in San Juan (see Domínguez 1975, 4). UCE is primarily composed of housewives not employed outside the home who are interested in civic and religious activities.[1] Most of the members are married to professionals and businessmen. In the mid 1980s UCE had 530 members on its roster as well as 60 *socios protectores* (sponsoring members), Cuban men who contributed financially to the organization. In June 1992 UCE's president estimated a membership of 650 (*El Nuevo Día,* June 24, 1992, 69). Additionally, UCE had some 80 members who contributed two hundred dollars every year to the association.

UCE is stronger in the San Juan metropolitan area than in other parts of the island. In 1984 members had organized seven neighborhood groups in San Juan and an eighth one in Arecibo. All the neighborhoods were middle- and upper-class areas with high concentrations of Cubans: Isla Verde, Miramar, Santa María, Santa Teresita, Torremolinos, Torrimar, and University Gardens. In 1991 UCE had additional neighborhood groups in Caparra Terrace, Garden Hills, Carolina, Los Paseos, and Villas de Torrimar. Although some Cuban women in Ponce have shown interest in UCE, a group has not yet been organized in that city.

Most of the association's funds come from members' quotas. In 1984 yearly quotas ranged from $36 to $60, depending on family income. Additionally, UCE conducts fund-raising activities not only to support the organization but also to promote good relations with the host society. In 1982 UCE organized an important cultural event called "Homage of Cuban Exiles to the People of Puerto Rico." The event consisted of an exhibit of the work of Cuban painters and sculptors residing in Puerto Rico, with the participation of Cuban and Puerto Rican intellectuals. Every year UCE collects between $16,000 and $28,000 to help needy Cuban exiles and Puerto Rican civic organizations (*El Reportero,* April 14, 1984). Between 1962 and 1991 UCE donated $457,353 to help Cuban exiles (UCE 1991). Most of the funds went to pay for food, lodging, education, funerals, medication, furniture, and airplane tickets. In September 1991 UCE spent $2,995 in public assistance (María Luisa Correa, personal interview, October 22, 1991).

UCE is an active organization. In 1983–84 its members sent blankets to recently exiled Cubans in Peru, participated in a conference on immigration to Puerto Rico, and sold tickets for a benefit raffle for the mentally retarded. The members also assisted the needy in the Puerto Rican community: they collected toys for poor children, organized a fashion show to benefit a home for the elderly, and bought presents for the sick. In 1990–91 UCE members organized a forum on the Mariel boatlift, a series of conferences on Cuban history, a talent show to benefit a school for blind children, and a prayer group. In 1991 UCE had tended to the needs of forty-two persons by October (María Luisa Correa, personal interview, October 22, 1991). Finally, UCE representatives participated in two activities sponsored by Puerto Rico's House of Representatives and Senate that protested against human rights violations in Cuba.

UCE participates regularly in Puerto Rico's campaigns against cancer, muscular dystrophy, and heart disease. Each year UCE donates a basketful of goods to a Puerto Rican mother who delivered her child on January 28, José Martí's birthday, and sponsors a mass in honor of Cuba's patron, Our Lady of Charity of Cobre, around September 8. UCE also helped a local hospital obtain a therapy room and a public school establish a library. According to the association's philosophy, "Every demand from the most needy must be heard in our work, and since we have received so much from this country, we must be generous in our giving" (UCE 1984).

UCE has been closely tied to the Catholic Church from its inception in

1962.[2] It was founded in Caracas, Venezuela, by the former assistant bishop of Havana, Monsignor Eduardo Boza Masvidal, with the purpose of "uniting, orienting, but above all helping Cubans in exile" (*El Reportero,* April 14, 1984). From Venezuela the association spread rapidly to Spain, Puerto Rico, Colombia, the United States, and Panama—almost anywhere the exiles went. UCE currently has seven principal centers in Miami, New Jersey, New York, San Juan, Los Angeles, Philadelphia, and Caracas. The central office is located in New Jersey.

Although the organization's primary orientation is civic and religious, UCE also endeavors to preserve the exiles' cultural identity. The bylaws of San Juan's chapter (UCE 1986) summarize the organization's main goals as follows: "(1) To reaffirm the Christian faith of Cubans residing in Puerto Rico; (2) To strengthen our civic consciousness through the preservation of values that constitute the national soul; and (3) To promote mutual aid between Cubans and Puerto Ricans." These goals are in close agreement with Boza's perception of UCE's main mission: "(1) To unite the dispersed Cubans and not allow physical dispersion to become spiritual dispersion; (2) To maintain the love for Cuba and preserve our culture and values; and (3) To learn solidarity through action, think of others, particularly the poorest, weakest, and neediest" (UCE 1983, 9–10). The first two goals are part of an effort to "keep alive the Cuban national spirit as it manifests itself through its cultural heritage and national traditions" (UCE 1983, 26). According to Boza, culture includes "our language, our religion, our history, our roots, our music, and our customs" (UCE 1983, 10).

A past president of UCE, Miriam Ben de López, emphasizes its political and religious components. In her view, UCE's fundamental purpose is to "organize Cuban exiles in a movement that will help bring about the restoration of freedom and democracy in Cuba" (UCE 1983, 25–26). She believes that UCE above all should strengthen fraternal links between Cubans and Puerto Ricans through mutual aid and that cultural preservation is a secondary task. Another former president, Sara Fernández, concurs: "What happens is that many of the younger people who come to UCE are not very interested in Cuban affairs" (personal interview, June 6, 1984). The association's main role is to attend to the material and spiritual needs of Cuban exiles. According to Fernández, UCE's core lies in its social assistance section. A third former president, María Luisa Correa, states that social assistance is the "backbone of the institution." She goes on to say : "UCE does not have a political character and abstains from taking sides on political issues pertaining to Cuban exiles" (personal interview, October 22, 1991).[3]

UCE's internal organization is the same in San Juan, Caracas, Miami, and New York. In each city UCE has a *directiva* (governing body) that is elected every two years. In the early years presidents were appointed by the directiva, but the practice has been discontinued and presidents are now elected. According to Fernández, officers are not really elected to be members of the directiva "because nobody wants to serve. One is pushed, manipulated into serving" (personal interview, June 6, 1984). Each city chapter comprises several committees and neighborhood areas. In 1991 San Juan's chapter included thirteen neighborhood subdivisions and three committees: Social Assistance, Religion, and Culture. There used to be separate male and female sections, but they merged in 1978, and women now preside over the organization. In the last three decades UCE has had several Catholic priests as spiritual advisers.

An excellent example of UCE's capacity to organize Cuban exiles in Puerto Rico occurred during the Mariel boatlift in 1980. That year the organization contributed $41,672 to help Cuban exiles, the highest sum in UCE's history. Most of the money went toward plane tickets: many Mariel refugees wanted to leave Puerto Rico but did not have money for the trip to Miami. According to Fernández, "The majority of the Marielitos are floating people; they don't stay put very long" (personal interview, June 6, 1984). Most of the Marielitos, however, did not have relatives in Puerto Rico, and the island's economic recession made jobs difficult to find. Be that as it may, UCE assisted about 760 Marielitos between 1980 and 1984 (Esteve 1984, 39). In 1980–81 UCE sent $16,000 to Cuban refugees in Costa Rica and Peru (UCE 1983, 25).

Since 1962 UCE has sponsored an annual mass in honor of the Lady of Charity. According to tradition, the Virgin Mary appeared to three sailors near Cuba's Nipe bay at the turn of the seventeenth century. Ever since then the Cuban people have worshipped the Virgin, proclaimed Cuba's patron saint in 1916. In September 1984 UCE organized a ceremony in honor of the Lady of Charity at a church in San Juan. Around one thousand persons were in attendance, mostly first-generation exiles and their children. Women were involved in every detail of the organization of the ceremony, ranging from the flower arrangement on the altar to taking up the collection, the latter usually being men's responsibility in Puerto Rico. Most people in attendance were well-dressed, healthy-looking, middle-aged whites.

The patriotic motif overrode the religious component of this event. The celebrant, Father Enrique Méndez, in his homily emphasized the contradiction between Catholic teaching and the communist system. Father Méndez's principal message was that the real Cuban values—God, fatherland, and family—were best preserved outside Cuba. After mass concluded, a lay speaker reaffirmed his faith that Cubans would return to their country to rescue Cuba from communism and turn it to Christianity and democracy. As a periodical published by Cuban exiles in the United States put it, "The image of our Lady of Charity . . . became in the heart of Cubans a symbol of Christian freedom against Communist atheism" (*El Mambí,* September 5, 1981).

In 1992 UCE commemorated thirty years of existence with a mass at a local church in San Juan. Father Boza himself, accompanied by other exiled Cuban priests, celebrated mass. Once again Father Enrique Méndez gave the homily, recalling the last three decades of UCE and forecasting its bright future. The central theme of his message was hope for an inminent return to Cuba. Prominent members of Puerto Rico's Cuban community—such as Leví Marrero, Himilce Esteve, and Anita Arroyo—took part in the celebration, which was attended by around one thousand persons.

UCE: An Anthropological Interpretation

The Unión de Cubanos en el Exilio serves a dual function in Puerto Rico. On the one hand, it channels the resources of the more affluent and better-established members to the less affluent and recently arrived. As a UCE booklet points out, "The generalized myth that the Cuban exile community consists mostly of economically successful individuals overshadows the reality of a large concentration of exiles who experience serious economic difficulties" (UCE 1991). In this sense UCE is a focus of ethnic identity that tends to blur class distinctions among Cubans and preserve cultural differences between Cubans and Puerto Ricans. On the other hand, UCE links the Cuban community with Puerto Rican society through a host of common civic activities. In this sense the organization projects a positive image of the exiles and fosters their integration into the receiving society. Every worthwhile fund-raising drive in Puerto Rico—whether to benefit the handicapped or the victims of hurricane Hugo—may count on UCE's help.

UCE undoubtedly helped the adaptation of Cuban exiles in Puerto Rico with economic and emotional support, particularly in the 1960s and 1970s, when many Cubans arrived with few contacts and resources. As Leví Marrero, a well-known Cuban intellectual in Puerto Rico, notes: "In Puerto Rico, nobody in twenty years has seen a destitute Cuban left at the mercy of public charity" (UCE 1983, 11).[4] UCE was in good measure responsible for the quick adaptation of Cubans in Puerto Rico.

Like the other major Cuban organization in San Juan, Círculo Cubano, UCE is fundamentally a vehicle for the exchange of resources within the immigrant community. From 1962 to 1991 UCE spent about 17 percent of its budget on services to the Puerto Rican community (UCE 1991). The remainder was spent on Cuban exiles. These data indicate, as Correa said, that UCE "is not concerned just with us [Cubans]" (personal interview, October 22, 1991). However, a clear line still divides Cubans and Puerto Ricans.

Hermandad de la Caridad: The Meaning of Cachita

So important is the Lady of Charity that Cubans in San Juan and cities in the United States have formed a religious sodality exclusively devoted to her.[5] Exiles formed this religious association because "being outside of Cuba, we feel a strong need to attach ourselves to those things that link us to the fatherland" (Hermandad de la Caridad 1983, 24). In the mid 1980s the San Juan sodality met once a month and sponsored a mass at a local church. Although a local parish priest, Father Nicanor Valdés, leads the association, its ultimate spiritual leader is Monsignor Boza. In principle, Hermandad de la Caridad is open to individuals of any nationality, but Cubans predominate. After all, Our Lady of Charity (or "Cachita," as some exiles affectionately refer to her) is as Cuban as Our Lady of Guadalupe is Mexican.

The association's most important event is a mass celebrated on the Lady of Charity's feast day, September 8.[6] In 1983 the mass was held at a stadium in Río Piedras. Due to a great deal of publicity, about three thousand persons were in attendance, the largest crowd of exiles in many years. The event's organizers distributed posters with the image of the Lady of Charity and the prayer "Our Lady of Charity, preserve our faith." As participants arrived, women pinned on them paper facsimiles of the Cuban flag, with an inscription at the bottom that said "Hermandad de la Caridad." Others sold copies of an Hermandad de la Caridad yearbook and passed out song sheets near the entrance. Inside the stadium a gigantic Cuban flag hung over the improvised altar. On one side stood an elaborate flower arrangement where the Virgin's image would later be placed; on the other side was a choir of young girls dressed in white and a musical group composed of men.

The ceremony began with the entrance of the priests and acolytes. The main celebrant was Luis Cardinal Aponte Martínez, archbishop of San Juan and a well-known friend of the exiles. Cardinal Aponte wore a chasuble with a likeness of the Cuban Republic's seal on its back. He was followed by a procession of believers carrying a statue of the Virgin as well as the flags of Cuba, Puerto Rico, the United States, and Hermandad de la Caridad. During the procession the audience sang a hymn to the Virgin: "Do not abandon, oh Mother, your people / Save Cuba from tears and troubles / And your name will be our shield / And your graces will be our refuge."

From the beginning of the ceremony, Cuban exiles were compared to Old Testament Jews. Scripture readings consistently emphasized the themes of exodus and persecution. The homily explicitly compared the Cuban and Hebrew diasporas and suggested that Cubans too were a chosen people and Cuba a promised land.[7] The preacher spoke of love of "God, the Gospel, fatherland, and family." He exhorted his audience to have faith and hope of returning to Cuba one day, and to practice charity while they waited. This interpretation of Catholic beliefs fits well with the experiences of many people who have spent more than thirty years in exile.

Under the theme "Lady of Charity, save Cuba," around five hundred Cubans went to the Fátima Church in Hato Rey in September 1991 to celebrate the feast day of the Virgin. Masses in honor of the Lady of Charity in Puerto Rico began in this church in 1960. On this occasion the homily was delivered by Father Avelino Fernández, a Cuban missionary serving on the border between Haiti and the Dominican Republic. His talk was much less patriotic than previous homilies. The priest stated that the fall of communism in Cuba would not mean the disappearance of sin from the world, and he urged the audience to reflect about its Christian faith and social consciousness. Even so, the ceremony included several allusions to the Cuban diaspora, such as prayers for Cubans who left their homeland in rafts. At the conclusion of the mass the choir sang in honor of the Lady of Charity. One of the songs had the following refrain: "All your children / Clamor to thee / Most Cuban Virgin / That we all may be brethren." Later, organizers placed yellow flowers before the Virgin's image. Finally, the audience sang the Cuban national anthem.

The next day Hermandad de la Caridad sponsored a second mass in honor of the Virgin. Over one thousand persons attended the ceremony at the Saint Therese Church in Santurce. The church was completely full; some of those in attendance had to stand. The ceremony began with the display of the flags of the United States, Puerto Rico, Cuba, and the Lady of Charity.

After the procession of thirteen priests, a group of exiles carried a statue of the Virgin, encircled by yellow flowers, to the altar. Members of the audience waved white handkerchiefs in token of their devotion to the Virgin. Father Avelino Fernández celebrated mass and delivered the homily. His sermon contained the same basic message delivered the previous evening: it is necessary to reaffirm the faith regardless of what happens in Cuba. As occurred the previous evening, participants said the Lord's Prayer while holding hands. Prints with the Virgin's likeness were distributed. On the backs of some was the prayer "May peace and love become again the heritage of the Cuban people"; other prints contained the prayer "Crush soon the head of the red serpent that torments our Fatherland." At the conclusion of the mass members of the audience clapped when a priest said that he hoped to observe the Virgin's feast day in Cuba the next year. They cheered "Long live the Lady of Charity! Long live Free Cuba!"

From an anthropological perspective, "ritual serves as the mechanism for maintaining opposition and thus becomes [the] focus of identity" of enduring ethnic groups (Castile and Kushner 1981, xx). As Edward Spicer and other anthropologists point out (Royce 1982), ethnic persistence implies the manipulation of shared symbols. In this sense, the mass in honor of the Lady of Charity dramatizes the abyss between Cubans in exile and those who support the revolution, between believers and nonbelievers. In invoking the myth of the lost fatherland, Hermandad reaffirms the origins of the ethnic group. In appealing to a sacred figure, Hermandad legitimates the exiles' moral values. By these means Cubans in Puerto Rico represent a spiritual community that is distinct from the receiving society.

Santería: A Minority Subculture

Another religious tradition followed by Cubans in Puerto Rico is *santería,* a popular religion that combines African (predominantly Yoruba) traditions and Spanish Catholicism. Outside Cuba santería is widely practiced wherever Cubans have settled in large numbers: Miami, New Jersey, New York, Chicago, Los Angeles, and San Juan. In Puerto Rico this Afro-Cuban religion expanded with the massive arrival of Cuban exiles in the 1960s. Originally the *santeros* (followers of santería) relied on *babalawaos* (priests) who traveled from New York on weekends to initiate believers. By the mid 1980s Puerto Rico had sixteen major babalawaos, eight of them Cuban exiles.[8]

A recent interview with a leading babalawao confirms the impact of Cuban immigration on the development of santería in Puerto Rico (Roberto Boluffer, personal interview, February 26, 1993). Boluffer estimates that roughly 25,000 persons have been initiated into santería in Puerto Rico and that from 40,000 to 50,000 persons participate in this religion. When Boluffer first arrived in Puerto Rico, he found only one babalawao; in his opinion, santería did not exist as an organized cult on the island. "The strong development of santería," he asserted, "started after the influx of Cubans to Puerto Rico."

Boluffer founded the first Yoruba temple in Santurce during the 1960s. He now presides over the Templo Yoruba Omo Orisha. He has personally initiated twenty-five priests, mostly Puerto Ricans, some Cubans, and other foreigners. His wife, a priestess, has initiated another sixty persons. Boluffer has tended to so many personal cares that he cannot be sure about the number of godchildren he has in Puerto Rico. The babalawao couple lives comfortably in a plush suburb of San Juan.

Today the Yoruba Omo Orisha Temple in Guaynabo, part of the San Juan metropolitan area, has around seven thousand followers. Dozens of *botánicas* (stores that sell herbs and other religious items used by santeros) have opened for business throughout the area. In sum, santería is an important aspect of Cuban culture in San Juan.

In 1983 the Yoruba Temple celebrated its New Year's ceremony with the assistance of twenty-one babalawaos and about two hundred believers. The ceremony lasted three days, from December 30 to January 1. The ceremony's main purpose was to announce the prophecies of the babalawaos for the coming year. The priests warned that Puerto Rico should be prepared to cope with a natural disaster such as a hurricane or earthquake during 1984. Additionally, they recommended that people guard against disease, keep their families united, and not do evil to anyone, especially through witchcraft (*El Reportero,* June 1–2, 1984). These warnings and recommendations were arrived at through an elaborate religious ritual called *Ifá.*

Julio Sánchez, who has studied Afro-Caribbean religions extensively, has suggested that most santeros in Puerto Rico belong to the middle or lower-middle class and that most, though not all, are mulatto or black (personal communication, September 9, 1983). Sánchez also reports that worship centers range from humble homes to luxurious mansions. There are at least four variations of santería in Puerto Rico. At the upper levels of the cult are the wealthiest babalawaos and their godchildren, who perform the most elaborate and expensive rituals of Afro-Cuban origin. At the lower levels santería becomes difficult to distinguish from spiritualism and other forms of popular religion in Puerto Rico. Several individuals have opened worship centers without the proper ritual knowledge, calling themselves santeros but having little in common with the religious system brought by Cubans to Puerto Rico. According to Puerto Rican anthropologist Ricardo Alegría, santería has had a strong impact on Afro–Puerto Rican religion, in part by commercializing it (personal communication, August 30, 1983).

A product of transculturation, Cuban santería has changed in exile. Much of the cult's core, however, has been preserved by Cubans in San Juan. For example, the names of the medicinal herbs used in rituals are Cuban, not Puerto Rican, and divinatory practices such as *opelé* and *dilogún* closely resemble those of prerevolutionary Cuba (Sánchez 1978). As in Miami and other Cuban communities in the United States, santería in San Juan provides a symbolic link with the past and a hope for the future (Sandoval 1979). Many exiles will call on a babalawao in search of emotional security when their children get sick, their parents die, their lovers stray, or their fortunes dwindle. Although most Cuban exiles are still baptized and get married within the Catholic Church, many try to meet their daily needs by turning to Changó and Yemayá, the two main Afro-Cuban deities.

Despite santería's popularity in many sectors of Puerto Rico's Cuban community, to be a santero means to belong to a minority subculture (Sánchez 1978). The majority of exiles consider santería a mixture of superstition and witchcraft, tarnished with the stigma of African culture, the black race, the lower class, and poor education. Racial prejudice and religious discrimination account in part for santería's marginal position in Puerto Rico's Cuban community. Another important reason is that santería's beliefs do not uphold the middle-class, mainstream values upheld by the dominant elements of the Cuban community. The cult is publicly rejected by the Cuban elite, overwhelmingly identified with the Catholic Church, though many may rely on babalawaos in moments of spiritual need.[9]

The Cuban-American National Foundation: The Antidote to Castro's Cuba?

Unlike the exiles' religious organizations, the Cuban-American National Foundation is openly political in nature. It was created in 1981 by a group of prosperous Cuban businessmen in the United States and Puerto Rico to "preserve freedom in the United States and return it to Cuba." The Puerto

Rico chapter was established in 1985 and currently has twenty-two directors and trustees (*El Nuevo Día,* May 20, 1992, S-4). One of the foundation's main achievements was the creation by the U.S. government of Radio Martí in 1985 and TV Martí in 1990, both of which broadcast to Cuba from Florida (Boswell and Curtis 1984, 172). The foundation also supported the Caribbean-basin policies of Presidents Reagan and Bush and worked closely with the State Department to disseminate public information on Latin America. Additionally, the foundation has published dozens of pamphlets condemning Castro's socialist regime. Today the foundation is the best-financed conservative Cuban organization in the United States. It was also the most influential Cuban organization with past Republican administrations (Fernández 1987). Currently the foundation has about ten thousand members in the United States (Jorge et al. 1991, 91).

On May 20, 1984—the anniversary of the beginning of the Cuban Republic—the Cuban-American National Foundation broadcast a program on Puerto Rican television. The program showed President Reagan and Florida senator Paula Hawkins congratulating the foundation for its efforts to promote democracy in Cuba. The program showcased President Reagan's 1983 visit to Miami's Little Havana, where he was received by more than a hundred thousand exiles. On that occasion the president praised the foundation as the "antidote to the great lie of Castro's Cuba." The remainder of the television program summarized Cuban nineteenth-century history. A Cuban exile in San Juan protested in a letter to a local newspaper that "the patriotic sequence was interrupted when the promotion of President Reagan's policies started, without a doubt in complete support of his reelection campaign" (*El Reportero,* June 4, 1984).

The Cuban-American National Foundation is a prime example of the incorporation of Cuban exiles to partisan politics in the United States. Although many Miami Cubans do not belong to the Republican Party, many sympathized with the anticommunist rhetoric of Reagan and Bush. Prominent members of the San Juan Cuban community—such as Arturo Barreiro, Eduardo Camejo, Jerónimo Esteve, Héctor Pagés, and Rafael Pratts—have been members of the foundation's board of directors. Such participation suggests that some wealthy Cubans in Puerto Rico have established close links with conservative leaders in Miami and Washington.

Although the impact of Cubans on Puerto Rican elections is minimal, their influence as a pressure group has grown in the last decade. In July 1991 the Senate of Puerto Rico passed a resolution giving recognition to the work of the Cuban-American National Foundation and its president, Jorge Más Canosa. The Senate expressed solidarity with the demand for a democratic referendum to return democracy to Cuba (*El Nuevo Día,* August 14, 1991). Some exiles in Puerto Rico protested the Senate's resolution on the grounds that the foundation does not represent the interests of the Cuban community but rather its conservative element (*Disidente,* August 1991).

On May 20, 1992, the foundation sponsored the publication of a special supplement to the newspaper *El Nuevo Día,* which "celebrated the 90th anniversary of the constitution of a free, sovereign, and democratic Cuban Republic." The cover displayed the drawing of a dove with the flags of Cuba, the United States, and Puerto Rico. An article by Jorge Más Canosa expressed his "conviction that the dismemberment and rotting of the Communist Cuban government are irreversible processes" (S-2). Other pieces in the supplement discussed the achievements of the foundation in its struggle to overthrow Castro. Among other things, the foundation had successfully lobbied the legislatures of Puerto Rico, Venezuela, and the Dominican Republic for resolutions condemning Cuba's socialist regime. Although the foundation does not perform as vital a function in Puerto Rico as it does in the United States, it represents an important advocacy group for Cuban exile business owners.

The Antonio Maceo Brigade: Heroes or Villains?

In comparison with the Cuban-American National Foundation, the Antonio Maceo Brigade lies on the opposite extreme of the political spectrum. This group represents a small radical minority of Cubans in the United States and Puerto Rico that emerged in the late 1960s (*Areíto* 1979, vol. 5, no. 19–20; Grupo Areíto 1978). In the mid 1980s around three hundred young exiles belonged to the Antonio Maceo Brigade. As an editorial in the magazine *Areíto* explained, "From the beginning, members of the Brigade thought of themselves as a group of young Cubans who bore no responsibility for their departure from Cuba. . . . Members were not required to agree with the ideology of the revolutionary process, but were expected to reject violence as a means of settling disagreements." According to one of the group's publications, its main goal is "to know personally the reality of today's Cuba . . . and to work actively for better relations with Cuba." Another important goal is "to strengthen the ties between Cubans living abroad and in Cuba," which is quite different from the main objective of other

Cuban organizations, which emphasize intensifying ties only among Cuban expatriates.

Since 1978 the Antonio Maceo Brigade's most important activity has been to organize an annual contingent of young exiles who visit Cuba for three weeks. Once in Cuba, the youngsters perform voluntary agricultural and construction work, visit historical sites, attend conferences on Cuban issues, and visit relatives. The trip to Cuba of the Antonio Maceo Brigade members was one of the most divisive issues in the Cuban exile community during the 1980s. Yet not all who traveled with the contingent were pro-Castro. Travel to Cuba with this group has five requirements (Brigada Antonio Maceo 1983b): 1) to have left Cuba as a minor or to have been born abroad of Cuban parents; 2) not to have participated in counterrevolutionary (i.e., anti-Castro) activities; 3) to support the end of the U.S. economic blockade against Cuba; 4) to support the normalization of relations between Cuba and the United States; and 5) to reject violence and terrorism against Cuba and Cubans abroad. These conditions exclude the right-wing sector of the Cuban exile community from the contingent, but they allow a wide variety of ideological positions, from middle-of-the-road liberal to extreme left. As members of the 1977 Antonio Maceo Brigade declared, "To visit Cuba, however, does not constitute an act of unconditional support to the Cuban Revolution nor a public proclamation in favor of socialism" (*Areíto* 1978, vol. 4, no. 3–4, p. 5).

The Antonio Maceo Brigade played an important role, together with various liberal sectors of the Cuban exile community, in the "Dialogue" of 1978 (Casal 1979; Torres 1988). The Dialogue was the first time that representatives of the Cuban government and the Cuban community abroad met to discuss matters of common interest, particularly family reunification and political prisoners. As a result of these conversations, more than a hundred thousand exiles traveled to Cuba in 1979 to visit their relatives, and close to three thousand political prisoners were allowed to leave Cuba. The Dialogue broke the myth of an exile community monolithically opposed to any negotiation with the Castro regime.[10] At the same time, the Dialogue resulted in an unprecedented wave of terrorism in the Cuban exile community. In 1979 one of the Antonio Maceo Brigade leaders, who was also president of Viajes Varadero, a travel agency specializing in trips to Cuba, was killed in San Juan (Argüelles and McEoin 1982). Although a right-wing organization claimed responsibility for the act, the case remains unsolved. In October 1991 the current president of Viajes Varadero, Raúl Alzaga, received a death threat from a Cuban exile organization, "Comando Cero."

The Antonio Maceo Brigade's significance must be seen in light of the growing political pluralization of Cuban exiles in the last three decades (Azicri 1982). A document titled "Puntos de unidad del V Contingente" shows how far members deviate from conservative exiles:

> We recognize the revolutionary process of the Cuban people as an irreversible historical fact. We maintain the necessity of deepening the permanent dialogue between the Cuban community living abroad and the Cuban government. We are opposed to the bellicose and interventionist policies of the U.S. government in Central America and the Caribbean. (Brigada Antonio Maceo 1983a)

These statements would be considered liberal, not radical, in the United States. However, the extreme right wing of the Cuban exile community considers them subversive. To belong to the Brigada Antonio Maceo means to be ideologically at the margin of the Cuban community in Miami and San Juan.

Who are the members of the Antonio Maceo Brigade, and what do they represent for the Cuban community of Puerto Rico? The founding members were between eighteen and thirty years old. Most originated from the better-educated strata of the middle class. A 1970 sample showed that more than half of the members were students or professionals. Eighty-eight percent were college graduates.[11] In 1988 the Antonio Maceo Brigade for the first time included Marielitos in the contingent (see editorial, *Areíto* 1988, vol. 1, no. 4).

Brigade members live in the major Cuban communities of the United States, Puerto Rico, Venezuela, Mexico, and Spain. They support such causes as the independence of Puerto Rico and repudiate others such as the U.S. invasion of Grenada and Panama. In 1980 members opposed the transfer of Cuban and Haitian refugees to Fort Allen in Juana Díaz, Puerto Rico. Some have lent "critical support" to the Cuban revolution, a position that has earned them the reputation of being infiltrated agents of the Castro government. Brigade members are clearly the enemies of right-wing groups such as Abdala and Omega 7, and several publications document their political antagonism.[12]

As we will see in the next chapter, the journal *La crónica* waged a verbal war with the handful of Antonio Maceo Brigade members who lived in Puerto Rico in the 1980s. However, as Azicri points out, "what seems to lie at the heart of the Brigade phenomenon is a more pervasive issue than any of its political postures and goals. It is the identity crisis felt by many Cuban-American youth" (1982, 63; see also Rumbaut 1984). Romano points out that the Antonio Maceo Brigade "is representative of a considerable group of members of the second generation who keep their Cuban identity more or less defined and are torn between the nostalgia of childhood, curiosity, and sympathy toward the revolutionary government" (1989, 82).

Conclusion

This chapter has shown that voluntary associations are a central axis of the Cuban community of Puerto Rico. The proliferation of formal organizations within the Cuban community provides a channel for information flux and for the establishment of interpersonal contacts among the exiles. Moreover, voluntary associations have helped the adjustment of Cubans in Puerto Rico, just as they have in West New York (Rogg and Cooney 1980, 74). Immigrant voluntary associations form a bridge between the homeland and the receiving society. For Cuban exiles in Puerto Rico, as Esteve states, "These associations have a common emphasis on keeping alive the memory of the fatherland through the commemoration of significant dates in Cuba's historical evolution, principally those related to the struggle for independence from Spain" (1984, 73–74).

The key function of the associations discussed in this chapter is to extend bonds of solidarity and cohesion among Cubans beyond the home in order to create a sense of community.[13] The main associations of the Cuban community of Puerto Rico, such as the UCE, Hermandad, and the Cuban-American National Foundation, expound political, religious, and moral values typical of a petite bourgeoisie. Additionally, the charity work of organizations such as the Unión de Cubanos en el Exilio helps propagate a positive image for the Cuban community in Puerto Rico. As a middleman group, Cubans are aware of negative stereotypes against them and try to combat them.

Not all Cuban organizations in Puerto Rico echo the values propounded by the group's petite bourgeoisie. Santería groups and the Antonio Maceo Brigade are examples of such organizations. But their departure from middleman group ideology helps explain their marginal status in the Cuban community. Although support of the values and ideas of the Cuban business class in Puerto Rico is not essential for organizations to exist, it is required for them to prosper.[14]

Although the future is uncertain, associations such as Casa Cuba and UCE have proven to be important institutions in the past. Perhaps they will eventually disappear, merging completely into Puerto Rican society. Or perhaps they will subsist as long as Cubans persist in the middleman role. Something similar is likely to happen to the Cuban press in Puerto Rico, to which we turn our attention in the next chapter.

8

The Cuban Press in Puerto Rico

The ethnic press plays a key role in the adaptation of many immigrants, middleman groups in particular. First, the ethnic press circulates information about the receiving society as well as the homeland. Second, the ethnic press promotes ethnic solidarity by upholding the culture and native language of the middleman group. Third, it combats negative stereotypes and promotes a positive image for the group. All of these activities support the economic specialization, cultural identity, and self-defense of middleman groups (Bonacich and Modell 1980; Bonacich et al. 1980, 176; Zenner 1991).

Although the Cuban media are not as extensive in San Juan as in Miami,[1] they constitute a significant force for two reasons. First, the Cuban presence in the Puerto Rican press is important. Many influential journalists are of Cuban origin, such as Carlos Castañeda and Chú García, former editors of the newspaper *El Nuevo Día;* Adolfo Comas Bacardí, former president of the *San Juan Star;* and Enrique Pizzi, the owner of the magazine *Vea.* Cubans have also had an important impact on the television, radio, and advertising industries. Second, Cuban exiles have produced numerous social, religious, and political publications for the in-group. Socially oriented publications include *Casa de Cuba,* the magazine of Círculo Cubano; *Vida de club,* published in Miami but containing much information about Cubans in Puerto Rico; and *Anuario de familias cubanas en el exilio,* a kind of international social register of the Cuban exile community.[2] The weekly column "Cuba y Puerto Rico son . . . ," which appeared in the now defunct daily *El Mundo,* also belongs in this category. The two main civic-religious publications are the yearbooks of the Hermandad de la Caridad and the Unión de Cubanos en el Exilio. Finally, the political press is represented by *La Crónica,* the most consistent Cuban tabloid in San Juan; *CID,* the official organ of the organization Cuba Independiente y Democrática; and *Areíto,* a left-wing magazine published originally in New York and later in Miami.[3]

This chapter analyzes a cross section of the Cuban press in Puerto Rico. It will identify the publications' recurrent themes as reflections of cultural values and social relations among the Cuban community. We hope to show how the exiles' middleman position becomes translated into the public ideology of a petite bourgeoisie.

La Crónica: "A Watchful Voice for Democracy"

In the early 1980s *La Crónica* held a virtual monopoly over conservative Cuban public opinion in Puerto Rico. Its predominant viewpoint was similar to that of Miami's *Diario de las Américas* (Aguirre 1979, 163). Founded in 1977, *La Crónica* is the successor to *Réplica,* whose editor was assassinated under mysterious circumstances. In the 1980s the owner of *La Crónica* was Antonio de la Cova, a former Cuban political prisoner convicted in Florida for illegal transportation of explosives; the editor was Gloria Gil, then de la Cova's wife. Since 1991 the tabloid has been published in Miami by new owners under the title *Crónica News,* but it still widely circulates in Puerto Rico.

La Crónica is distributed free in places frequently attended by Cubans: restaurants, cafeterias, bakeries, supermarkets, and clubs.[4] It is financed by the sale of commercial advertising, mainly to Cuban businesses. Its editorial line is openly belligerent to Cuban communism and its "international net of agents" (*La Crónica,* September 1983). Its tone and rhetoric may be appreciated in the following quotation: "Writing a press note, drafting a text, attending a revolutionary event, preparing a march or protest, are important things [in the political struggle] but much more important is to strike hard, whenever possible, at the dens of the direct representatives of Communist imperialism and the offices and sections of its most despicable lackeys" (*La Crónica,* September 1983).

The contents of *La Crónica*—like those of *Patria* in Miami and *Ultima Hora* in New York—are a mixture of investigative journalism, police mystery, fashion reports, political manifestos, and media hype. One editorial supports anti-Castro terrorist acts, another condemns a young Cuban exile dissident as an "infiltrated agent" from Cuba, and a third one attacks moderate elements of the exile community for having betrayed the ideals of the

Cuban patriot José Martí. The theme of betrayal permeates the pages of *La Crónica,* obsessed with keeping a united front and castigating anyone who deviates from its view of political orthodoxy. At the same time, the tabloid is full of trivial information, such as reports on beauty contests, beauty tips, and articles on topics such as whether television star Lourdes Chacón used silicone implants to increase the size of her breasts. These sections seem to be designed to appeal to women. Politics has been traditionally dominated by men in the exile community.

La Crónica articulates the conservative ideology propounded by members of Puerto Rico's Cuban community, particularly its petite bourgeoisie. The tabloid echoes their complaints, hopes, and interests in the fatherland. *La Crónica* names the friends and enemies of the exile community, and more and more frequently the enemies are found within the exile community itself. It publicizes the stories of cultural heroes and the outrage perpetrated against them, such as the imprisonment in the United States of Eduardo Arocena, leader of Omega 7, a radical anti-Castro group, for the bombing of a Cuban airline. The tabloid uses national identity symbols to legitimate its worldview, not only in the political sphere but in the area of morals as well. In September 1983 the columnist *El centinela* (The Sentinel) attacked several homosexual exiles who supported the Cuban revolution. A few months later, in March 1984, another article riled against a small group of "effeminate [men] and butch [women]" intellectuals who had attended a "Castroite encounter" at a university in Puerto Rico. *La Crónica* not only defends conservative politics but also leads a crusade against the transgression of conventional sexual norms. Its editors are staunch opponents of any form of social deviance.

The image of the *madre patria* (motherland) is the axis of the publication. *La Crónica* advocates a free Cuba "where there is no exploitation, neither of man by man, nor of man by the state (*La Crónica,* August 1983). Its editors promote the return to an idealized prerevolutionary Cuba—*la Cuba del ayer.* To this end, they support extreme right-wing organizations such as Omega 7, Abdala, and Brigade 2506 because the editors "admire and respect those who sever with bullets the heads of communists, wherever they may be found" (*La Crónica,* September 1983).[5]

Three public incidents illustrate *La Crónica*'s role within the Cuban community. The first, which reached the pages of local newspapers, pertains to the case of Carlos Muñiz Varela, the leftist young exile murdered in San Juan in 1978. In April 1979 Omega 7 had assumed responsibility for the killing (Torres 1988, 88). In the summer of 1984 *La Crónica* published a series of front-page photographs of Muñiz's autopsy. His widow sued the periodical on the grounds that the pictures were private and confidential, and that they had been obtained illegally. *La Crónica*'s attorney was Sergio Ramos, a member of Abdala. The court ruled in favor of the tabloid because Muñiz and his wife had become public figures and as a consequence were "not entitled to privacy" (*La Crónica,* October 1984). Muñiz's corpse had become a battleground between opposing political factions. The resolution of the case prompted a celebration among *La Crónica* sympathizers at a Cuban restaurant in San Juan.

The second incident was related to the television program *Los suegros y los nietos* (The In-laws and the Grandchildren), a popular weekly comedy broadcast in Puerto Rico and the United States. The series featured a Cuban exile couple and their son and his wife, who was Puerto Rican. The conflicts between the two sets of in-laws were the focus of the comedy. The Puerto Rican father-in-law despised his Cuban counterpart. The Cuban father-in-law, Ñico, always wore a *guayabera* (Cuban shirt), a straw hat, and a golden medallion around his neck. His wife wore expensive clothes, and her hair was dressed elegantly. Both characters embodied the stereotype of the arrogant, loquacious, and party-loving Cuban.

In the mid 1980s *La Crónica* conducted a campaign to get the program off the air on the grounds that it ridiculed Cubans in Puerto Rico. In March 1984 *La Crónica* bestowed the program's main protagonist and scriptwriter, Manuel Montero, the title of *Guanajo del mes* (Turkey of the Month). In September 1984 *La Crónica* published several interviews with Cubans regarding the program. Not surprisingly, most of the responses were negative. The editors of *La Crónica* concluded that the program "blackens the image of the hard-working Cuban, offering us a medallion-wearing Cuban, who is ill-mannered, boastful, and ostentatious" (March 1984). In October 1984 the editors summed up their own way of thinking about their compatriots:

> Cuban exiles in Puerto Rico have at all times behaved exemplarily, except on rare occasions, as happens everywhere. They have been able to live in harmony, and with respect and honesty, within Puerto Rican society. They have established their homes here. They have started businesses where many Puerto Rican fathers earn their living, and in general have contributed to the greatness of all socioeconomic and cultural areas of this country, while at the same time, of course, forgetting neither their own roots

> nor the subjugated Fatherland. And, false modesty aside, they have contributed positively [to Puerto Rico] as no other ethnic group has.

The third incident occurred in 1991, when members of the Cuban exile community sent an open letter to President Bush. The letter's purpose was to "defend the Cuban people's right to fight for freedom." In a long editorial *La Crónica* pointed out that, because 250,000 exiles signed the open letter, the belligerent position of the letter represented "the almost unanimous position of the Cuban exile community." The editorial went on to say:

> We do not wish to elude our commitment with the Cuban people to support human rights. Our core values, however, go beyond simple respect for human rights. We intend, and are fully committed to do so, to eradicate for ever the system that so oppresses our people. . . . Any attempt at an understanding with the tyrant [Castro], even a supposed opening to greater democracy, would only contribute to the perpetuation of communism in power. (1992, vol. 1, no. 7)

In sum, *La Crónica* and its successor, *Crónica News,* present themselves as the only legitimate exponents of Cuban exile public opinion in the United States and Puerto Rico. *La Crónica* opposes peaceful coexistence between Cuba and the United States as well as the normalization of relations between the two countries. Moreover, the tabloid fights against negative stereotypes against Cubans on Puerto Rican television and newspapers and promotes the group's positive image. Last, the magazine defends a free-enterprise ideology characteristic of the petite bourgeoisie. However, political diversity has increased in the last twenty years in the exile community (Azicri 1982; Fernández 1987; Torres 1988). As will be shown, other Cuban exile publications in Puerto Rico and the United States express more-liberal and even radical points of view.

CID: The Liberal Tradition

Since 1981 the anti-Castro organization Cuba Independiente y Democrática (CID) has published the newspaper *CID.* Politically *CID* is to the left of *La Crónica* and to the right of *Areíto.* This publication was started in Caracas by Húber Matos, a former comrade-in-arms of Castro who spent twenty years in Cuban prisons for opposing the revolution's turn to Marxism. Matos currently resides in Miami but keeps in touch with his exile followers in San Juan and elsewhere.

In December 1991 thirty-five thousand copies circulated free of charge through seventy-five delegations throughout the United States, Puerto Rico, Latin America, and Europe. Although *CID* is published in Miami, its articles are international in scope and frequently deal with Puerto Rico. In July 1983 the newspaper had reports on the Dominican Republic, Nicaragua, Venezuela, El Salvador, Puerto Rico, the United States, and Cuba. In December 1991 *CID* carried news about Argentina, Italy, France, Costa Rica, Poland, the Canary Islands, Canada, and other countries. *CID* supported former president Reagan's policy toward Central America. It operates four radio stations that broadcast to Cuba and attempts to undermine the Castro government through peaceful means.

Like Miami's *Réplica, CID* represents the liberal wing of the Cuban exile community, made up largely of middle-class professionals, intellectuals, and businesspersons who initially supported the revolution but became disenchanted when it became more radical and embraced socialism. Montaner calls this sector the "democratic left" of the exile community:

> Curiously, there are more former leaders of the revolution against Batista living in Puerto Rico than in any other [Cuban] migration center. There are tens of former guerrilla officers, underground leaders, and political personalities. Although the origins of the migration that concentrated in Miami may be traced back to pre-revolutionary days, the mark of the migrant stream to San Juan is best described—within the ideological confines of the Cuban exodus—as "betrayed revolution." (1971, 10)

CID differs from *La Crónica* in four fundamental ways. First, *CID* does not advocate an exile armed struggle to liberate Cuba but supports an internal rebellion as a necessary condition for the overthrow of Castro. Second, *CID* is published in Miami by a central committee of the organization, not by a group of private citizens, as is *La Crónica*. Third, *CID* has a much more international focus. Fourth, *CID* appeals to anti-Castro exiles who do not identify with Batista's dictatorship, while *La Crónica* does not repudiate Batista.

In 1991 the organization CID joined the anti-Castro organization Concertación Democrática Cubana, whose purpose is to unify exile anti-Castro dissidents with their counterparts in Cuba. Created in Havana in

September 1991, Concertación includes eleven political and human rights organizations inside and outside Cuba (*El Nuevo Herald,* September 11, 1991, 3A). The founding documents of Concertación point out the need to "satisfy the dreams of peace, national reconciliation, and true democracy of the people of Cuba." During one of the last annual meetings of CID in Miami, hundreds of delegates from the United States, Puerto Rico, Latin America, and Europe discussed the role of internal resistance in Cuba and political alliances with other exile political groups outside Cuba (*Diario Las Américas,* September 5, 1991, 5B). Historical conditions made it possible for CID and other Cuban exile organizations to set aside ideological differences and join in a common front against Cuban communism.

The secretary-general of CID, Húber Matos, is a controversial figure in the Cuban exile community. A former commander of a guerrilla column of Castro's 26th of July Movement, Matos resigned his position shortly after the triumph of the revolution because Castro's government was being infiltrated by communists. His resignation was seen as an act of treason, and Matos was sentenced to twenty years in prison. However, the conservative wing of the exile community in Miami shunned Matos because he was perceived as being too leftist. Matos nonetheless appeared wearing military garb while visiting Nicaraguan contras in the mountains of Central America. His five basic principles—national independence, political democracy, economic freedom, social justice, and integration with Latin America—reflect the populist and reformist spirit of the original July 26 movement in the 1950s. In the context of the Cuban exile community, CID is best characterized as left of center.

Areíto: "An Alternative Open to Dialogue"

Farther to the left than *CID,* the magazine *Areíto* sees the Cuban revolution as a necessary historical fact and proposes the reestablishment of diplomatic links between Cuba and the United States. With an initial edition of one thousand copies, the first issue of *Areíto* was sold out quickly in 1974. In starting the magazine, its editors created "a vehicle that has made clear [through its pages] the wide gamut of political positions existing in the exile community" (*Areíto,* April 1978). However, *Areíto* clearly defines itself as a "vehicle of the left" ("Editorial," vol. 4, nos. 3–4, 1978). From the publication of its first issue, the magazine attempted to present "a serious, though nonacademic, evaluation of today's Cuba: its economic and social policies, the life of its people and of its youth, its achievements and its failures" (*Areíto,* April 1974). For instance, a recent issue of the magazine examined popular religion in Cuba (vol. 1, no. 3, second epoch, 1988). In Miami, New Jersey, and San Juan the Cuban ethnic media reacted negatively to the publication of this magazine.

Most of *Areíto*'s founders were young Cuban students and university professors living in the United States and Puerto Rico, such as Lourdes Casal, Marifeli Pérez-Stable, Raúl Alzaga, and José Ramón Villalón. In the beginning the publishers of the magazine were interested mainly in the Cuban revolutionary process and Cuban exiles in the United States. Later magazine coverage expanded to other Latin American countries and other Hispanic groups in the United States (see *Areíto,* vol. 4, nos. 1–2, 1978). Through the years *Areíto* has published articles on Puerto Rico, Nicaragua, the Dominican Republic, Chile, Panama, and Brazil, among other countries. It has also devoted its attention to Mexican Americans and Puerto Ricans in the United States. But the magazine's main concern is Cuban culture, particularly literature and films, not only in Cuba but in exile as well. As a 1981 editorial asserts, *Areíto* attempts to serve as a "bridge between us, Cubans who from exile yearn for contact with the Fatherland's vital essence, and Cubans on the island who, firmly rooted in their own land, wish to enter a dialogue" (vol. 7, no. 25).

In retrospect, *Areíto*'s major impact was to initiate a dialogue between "progressive" elements inside and outside the Cuban exile community. Although such elements constitute a minority within the exile community, *Areíto*'s significance went beyond those in whom it found a sympathetic audience. For the first time a public voice disagreed with the Cuban ethnic media in Miami and San Juan. As one editorial put it, "For the first time, since 1978–79, one senses in Miami a popular opinion that challenges right-wing dogmas" (vol. 1, no. 4, second epoch, 1988). This challenge explains the ferocious campaign against *Areíto* undertaken by San Juan's *La Crónica* and other exile publications. Cuban exiles who oppose any rapprochement with Cuba's socialist regime deride *Areíto*'s posture as "dialoguist" and "Castroite." In any event, the existence of *Areíto* and kindred organizations, such as the Antonio Maceo Brigade, belies the apparent ideological uniformity of the Cuban exile community in the United States and Puerto Rico.

Casa de Cuba: Official Publication of the Círculo Cubano de Puerto Rico

With a focus more social than political, *Casa de Cuba* was one of the most consistent Cuban exile publications in Puerto Rico during the 1970s. The official publication of the Círculo Cubano de Puerto Rico, this periodical first appeared in 1972 with the purpose of "serving as a vehicle of unity between the members and the Executive Board" of the club ("Editorial," November 1973). Among other topics, the magazine has covered Mother's Day, the conclusion of the squash championship, the wedding of a young female member, and the graduation of a distinguished student. Articles usually include photographs of members socializing on important occasions. *Casa de Cuba* will sometimes contain historical pieces on the anniversary of the birth of José Martí or the Ten Year War of independence against Spain. The bulk of the articles, however, deal with sports and pastimes, such as dominoes, canasta, and bingo. The magazine pays special attention to the annual carnival, queens' crownings, and debutante balls.

The club's executive board endeavors to show through the pages of *Casa de Cuba* that "our modest contribution has made our *Círculo Cubano de Puerto Rico* an institution that brings honor to the exile community" (year 1, no. 7, 1972). As a result, the magazine promotes member participation in the club's social and sporting events, something that, not coincidentally, serves to generate support for the executive board. The increase in the number of members and the expansion of the club's facilities are recurrent themes of *Casa de Cuba*. Another is the conscious avoidance of taking sides in political disputes within Puerto Rico's Cuban exile community (see editorial, year 1, no. 11, 1972). These two themes reflect the magazine's efforts to integrate all members into a large family based on mutual respect and cooperation. Such a goal helps explain the magazine's constant use of personal notes and group photographs.

The magazine, however, can only go so far in trying to be apolitical. But when it deals with political issues, it does so carefully. A 1973 editorial invokes, "Cuba, beloved Fatherland which soon will reach the 15th anniversary of the establishment of slavery under the worst possible dictatorship that humanity has produced, atheist communism"; immediately the editorial directs a prayer to Our Lady of Charity: "May the mind of all Cubans see the light so that, setting aside all lowly ambitions, we will all reach a common goal: the return to Cuba we so long for" (November 1973). Thus, *Casa de Cuba* defines the ideology of exile in terms of patriotic fervor and Catholic devotion, two pillars of Cuban tradition.

Mixed in with the magazine's nationalism are excerpts pertaining to the club's daily life. Dances, parties, games, and tournaments alternate with historic dates and patriotic discourses. Social events, however, predominate. Although many editorials espouse an anticommunist rhetoric, most of the magazine's pages are devoted to the achievements of Cuban exiles in Puerto Rico in areas ranging from sports to business. The primary goal of *Casa de Cuba*, then, is to strengthen ethnic ties among the club's members, and a secondary goal is to promote the struggle against communism.

Vida de club and the Old Free Cuba

Like *Casa de Cuba, Vida de club* is principally concerned not with politics but with high society. Since its beginning in 1982, this monthly magazine has gathered information about the many Cuban social clubs in exile.[6] One of the 1982 issues (vol. 1, no. 5), features news on Miami's Big Five, Tampa's Club Cívico Cubano, Hialeah's Westland Country Club, and San Juan's Círculo Cubano. The articles cover mostly the social events of these clubs—dinners, parties, informal gatherings, and sports. They illustrate graphically the bonds that tie Cubans in San Juan with their compatriots in other areas, particularly U.S. cities. A 1984 editorial (vol. 3, no. 3) recognizes that the publication is based on photographs provided by the exiles themselves; the previous issue includes 222 such photographs. *Vida de club* also tries to appeal to those who are not lucky enough to appear on its pages. An appeal to readers goes as follows:

> Maybe you have a friend or relative outside Miami, in a state that does not have a club in the style of those we had in yesteryear's Free Cuba, like those we have in Miami, Fort Lauderdale, Puerto Rico, and Tampa. Why not keep them informed about our club activities. Give them a year's subscription to VIDA DE CLUB. It is a gift they will never forget.

Vida de club caters mainly to the Cuban elite of Miami, San Juan, and New York. Its expensive paper, high-quality print, color photographs, and full-page advertisements indicate that this is a magazine for the more economically advantaged segment of the exile community. *Vida de club* extols the lifestyle of Cuban exiles who belong to exclusive circles. The magazine nourishes a nostalgia for the past, when the pace of life was slower and surnames more important. In brief, *Vida de club* manifests a desire to maintain continuity among Cubans both in time and space. It seeks to bring together the members of the different clubs throughout the United States and Puerto Rico. And it attempts to maintain the links between the prerevolutionary past and the current exodus.

Anuario de familias cubanas: The Importance of Surnames

Published since 1967 in Puerto Rico and subsequently in Miami, the *Anuario de familias cubanas* continues the tradition of social registers of prerevolutionary Cuba, but it is not restricted to the exiles' elite. Rather, a family's inclusion depends primarily on whether it buys the yearbook or not. According to the yearbook's editor, Joaquín de Posada, its main purpose is to keep exile families in touch with each other, regardless of economic position. Still, the *Anuario* reflects the overrepresentation of upper- and middle-class families in exile. As the prologue to the 1973–74 edition states, "The *Anuario* is the register of Cuba's best . . . a panoramic overview of how Cubans triumph in foreign lands, in all areas, from the economic to the social and professional." Posada adds: "Cuban settlements around the world are like hives of industrious and untiring bees" (1973–74, 4). In edition Posada notes: "Cubans always distinguished themselves for their extraordinary industry and ability, their talent and comportment, all of which have placed them at the head of all who have had to emigrate for reasons similar to ours" (1979–80, 4).

The yearbook praises the family as the pillar of Cuban nationality because of its sense of spirituality, hospitality, and self-sacrifice. Posada goes beyond simple melancholy to lead a crusade for the preservation of Cuban customs. In 1977 he wrote that Cuban women should keep their own surnames when they marry: "Since we lost our fatherland and until we recover it, we should conserve our traditions."[7] Thus, married women are listed with both their father's and husband's surnames.

The *Anuario* lists a disproportionately large number of Cuban exiles living in Puerto Rico. Around 30 percent of all Cubans in San Juan appear in the 1973–74 edition (Cooney and Contreras 1978, 44). This overrepresentation suggests that the Cuban community of Puerto Rico enjoys a higher socioeconomic status than its counterparts in the United States. Moreover, Posada lived in Puerto Rico until recently and was in a better position to market the yearbook there than in the United States.

Cuba and Puerto Rico Are . . .

In the 1980s a weekly column titled "Cuba y Puerto Rico son" (Cuba and Puerto Rico Are) appeared in the newspaper *El Mundo*. The title was borrowed from a poem frequently cited by Cubans in Puerto Rico: "Cuba y Puerto Rico son / De un pájaro las dos alas / Y juntas reciben balas / En un solo corazón" (Cuba and Puerto Rico are / Like two wings of one bird / Together they receive bullets / Upon the same heart). These lines of verse written by Puerto Rican poet Lola Rodríguez de Tió inspired a Cuban exile, Dr. Andrés Garcés, to chronicle the historical, literary, and artistic events of San Juan's Cuban community.[8] Faithful to the column's title, he also commented on Puerto Rican cultural events. The author congratulated painters on their achievements, publicized literary contests, wrote biographical sketches on illustrious personages, and underlined the commonalities between Cuba and Puerto Rico. His views reached a wide Cuban and Puerto Rican audience who read *El Mundo*'s Sunday editions.

This column was basically an effort to promote Cuban cultural activities in Puerto Rico and cement "the sentimental links that unite our two countries." As Garcés saw it, Cubans identify emotionally with Puerto Ricans through a "profound cultural and civic compenetration between the two nations."[9] Thus the emphasis was on the social integration between Cubans and Puerto Ricans rather than on their cultural differences. No other newspaper column in Puerto Rico defended ethnic causes and values as much as "Cuba y Puerto Rico son" did. No other ethnic group—except North Americans—has had as much influence on the Puerto Rican mass media as Cubans have. This column exemplifies how Cuban exiles have articulated their interests before Puerto Rican society.

Anuario de la Caridad: Our Lady Again

The Hermandad de la Caridad, the Cuban religious sodality in San Juan, puts out a yearbook irregularly. The text is oriented toward Catholic orthodoxy, although the Lady of Charity is also revered in several Afro-Cuban cults, such as santería, that identify her with the African goddess Ochum. The yearbook presents the Virgin as the ideal model, "capable of being at all times the meeting point, source of consolation, refuge, and encouragement for all of her children." Her significance is related to her cultural and patriotic relevance: "Only the Virgin of Charity is able to maintain the Cuban people united; she is the undisputed link that ties us forever to our land" (Hermandad de la Caridad 1983). Without doubt, the Virgin of Charity represents the essence of national identity for the Cuban exile community.

The Lady of Charity symbolizes the values of motherhood, family, and fatherland. An article in the 1983 issue of the yearbook, "An Image which is a Symbol," sees the Virgin as the embodiment of traditional Cuban sex roles.

For women the Lady of Charity represents an "exquisite femininity, capable of mustering all the strength and abnegation required to satisfy fully her mission as woman and mother." For men the Lady signifies "spirituality and exaltation and a respect for women that will make them better gentlemen, more conscious of their responsibilities and mission, and thus more manly" (Hermandad de la Caridad 1983, 83). Thus, the Virgin symbolizes God's plan for male-female relations, above all between husband and wife. In sum, the yearbook expresses a vision of Cuban society rooted in the Catholic faith.

Global Analysis and Interpretation

Cuban exile publications in Puerto Rico have a common purpose: the preservation of traditional Cuban culture. *La Crónica* does it by promoting conservative political ideology, *Casa de Cuba* by celebrating the lifestyle of the middle and upper classes, and *Anuario de familias cubanas* and *Anuario de la Caridad* by espousing family codes and religious traditions. All of these publications tend to present an idealized version of the Cuban past. No one does this better than Bibi Arenas in *Anuario de la Caridad,* where she depicts Cuba as a tropical paradise, laden with palm trees, rivers, coffee, sugar, flowers, and fruit (Hermandad de la Caridad 1983, 127–29).

The desire to return to Cuba is not the only force behind these publications; there is also an economic incentive. The 1983 *Anuario de la Caridad,* for instance, includes an advertisement for as "the travel agency of Puerto Rico's Cuban colony. United we help each other. Try us and you will see!" The September 1983 issue of *La Crónica* touts a brand of cigars "manufactured in the Dominican Republic with the traditional quality of Cuban technicians." UCE's yearbook of 1983 lists more than forty Cuban firms in Puerto Rico, such as insurance agencies, jewelers, furniture stores, construction firms, restaurants, and supermarkets. Even the travel agency Marazul advertises in *Areíto* as the agency of "progressive professionals." Selling and buying is a central part of the Cuban experience in Puerto Rico, as is the case among other middleman groups. A basic motive in these publications is to promote ethnic businesses.

Exile publications are aimed primarily at the older immigrants who still remember prerevolutionary Cuba. The sole exception is *Areíto,* which focuses on the second generation of exiles. Political publications are aimed at men, while religious ones are directed at women. The majority of the publications, regardless of content, are targeted to a readership that is conservative on social, economic, and political matters. *Vida de club,* for example, promises its readers that it will never cover "conflictive or immoral issues." Another component of the audience implied in these publications is good taste. The readership includes a high proportion of managers, professionals, and technicians. It also includes a white population that likes to celebrate its Spanish and Creole origins.

With the exception of *Areíto,* the publications are unanimous in their praise of liberal democracy and free enterprise and in their condemnation of Castro's regime. Most of the publications agree on the following points: 1) Cuban exiles' economic success is based on hard work and personal sacrifice; 2) Cubans must maintain their faith in God and fatherland; 3) Cubans are grateful to the Puerto Rican people for their hospitality; 4) Cubans do not wish to isolate themselves from Puerto Rican society, but neither do they want to lose their national identity; 5) Cubans share three basic values—God, fatherland, and family; and 6) Cubans have two great national symbols: José Martí and Our Lady of Charity. In sum, Cuban exiles in Puerto Rico feel alienated from Castro's government but not from Cuba itself. The majority of the exiles continue to embrace the cultural values of prerevolutionary Cuba, centered on family, friendship, and individualism. The *Anuario de la Caridad* specifically mentions trust and respect as the core of Cuban culture (Hermandad de la Caridad 1983).

A primary objective of these publications is to achieve ideological consensus among the exiles.[10] With the exception of *Areíto,* all the publications depict Fidel Castro as a sort of anti-Christian figure in Cuban history. But when it comes to relating to the present environment, they are quite diverse. As Rumbaut notes, "The meaning of exile is interpreted in different ways by the expatriates, according to the generational and socioeconomic positions they occupy" (1984, 36).

Conclusion

The goal shared by the publications discussed in this chapter is to promote a sense of common origin and destiny among Cubans in Puerto Rico and the United States. The publications attempt to instill ethnic pride among the young exiles and to renew it among the older ones. They remind the exiles that they or their parents were born in a great country, that they descend from an illustrious line of men and women, and that they are part of an epic history of exodus and reconquest of the lost fatherland. They define Cubanness as a spirit of struggle, sacrifice, and progress before adversity. From this perspective, to be Cuban means to belong to a race of heroes and martyrs, rebels and idealists. Cuban exiles often compare themselves with the Jews, for they see themselves as a chosen people. To return to our point of departure, some Cubans like to think of themselves as the "Jews of the Caribbean."

Like other middleman groups, Cubans in Puerto Rico have used the ethnic press to support their cultural identity, economic specialization, and ocupational prestige. The Cuban exile press has been an important source of information about the fatherland and other compatriots. In this manner, the ethnic press has helped Cubans maintain their sense of worth and develop high achievement motivation. In sum, the Cuban press has promoted social solidarity and ethnic persistence among the exiles and defended their public image in Puerto Rico.

Conclusion

This book has examined the social and economic experiences of Cubans in Puerto Rico in light of middleman group theory. The purpose of this chapter is to synthesize the book's main arguments and assess their significance. We begin by summarizing the major characteristics of Cuban migration to the United States. We then review the middleman group model and recapitulate our findings on Cubans in Puerto Rico in light of it.

The Cuban Exodus

Fidel Castro's ascent to power in 1959 unleashed an unprecedented series of events in Cuban history. When Batista fell from power, the vast majority of the Cuban people supported the revolution. But when the new government began to reform society, sometimes through measures more radical than many had anticipated, popular discontent arose. Although the discontent began among the wealthy classes, it eventually reached persons of more modest means. Many of the dissatisfied individuals chose to leave, most settling in the United States.

The Golden Exile of the Cuban exodus began in 1959 and lasted until 1962, when the Cuban Missile Crisis developed. One fourth of the total Cuban migrant stream arrived in the United States during this period. The Missile Crisis interrupted migration of Cubans to the United States until the latter part of 1965, when the Cuban government opened the port of Camarioca for emigration. A few months after the opening of Camarioca, negotiations between the United States and Cuba resulted in the establishment of the Freedom Flights, which between 1965 and 1973 took a third of the total migrant stream. The social composition of the exiles began to change in the late 1960s and early 1970s. Although the more advantaged sectors of Cuban society were still overrepresented among the emigrants, their proportion had decreased.

The suspension of the Freedom Flights in April 1973 reduced Cuban migration considerably. In April 1980 the Cuban government opened up the port of Mariel, and in less than two months almost 125,000 Cubans departed for the United States. With the arrival of Marielitos—many of them young, single, black or mulatto, modestly educated, working-class men—the exile population became more representative of Cuba's population. In the 1990s, the Cuban exodus reached levels comparable to the Mariel boatlift, drawing on an ever growing variety of sectors of Cuban society.

While many U.S. cities have Cuban settlements, the bulk of the exiles settled in the Miami metropolitan area. In Miami the exiles established an economic structure that Portes and his collaborators have dubbed the "ethnic enclave." Such a structure comprises a network of firms that serve an in-group clientele. A smaller and more select portion of the Cuban migrant stream settled in Puerto Rico, principally in the San Juan metropolitan area. These immigrants have followed a different strategy from that of their compatriots in Miami. Cubans in Puerto Rico play the same middleman role that in other contexts has been performed by Quakers and Scots in the United States and Canada, Germans in Imperial Russia, and overseas Chinese in several countries.

Middleman Groups

The study of middleman groups has been dominated by the classic model proposed by scholars such as Weber and Simmel. The classic model constitutes an ideal type. Ideal types are abstract models that accentuate some traits of social phenomena for comparative analysis.

According to the classic model, middleman groups are permanently wandering peoples who settle in nonindustrialized societies. Middleman group members tend to be better off than the bulk of their hosts. Their command of foreign languages and international contacts make them adept at commerce and finance. In addition to their business acumen, middleman groups possess a sojourning mentality that prompts them to invest in liquid pursuits such as trade and avoid immovable investments such as manufacture. The business opportunities for middleman groups occur in traditional societies because elite members will not, for reasons of status, trade with the lower classes. Middleman groups take advantage of such status gaps and serve the lower classes, as a result becoming useful to the elite. That is why middleman groups receive certain privileges from the elite. Ironically, elites also discriminate against middleman groups, denying them access to certain occupations.

Classic middleman groups are clannish and prefer to relate with and marry other coethnics. Group members who are not self-employed work for coethnics. Middleman groups preserve their own language and religion, and they stand apart from the receiving society because of their customs, diet, or mode of dress. Their businesses follow precapitalist practices in many areas, such as employer-worker relations, which are based on trust and loyalty.

Because of their economic success, clannishness, and reputation as shrewd businessmen, middleman groups provoke antagonism and discrimination from the host society. That is why the classic model refers to them as middleman minorities. In an effort to deviate public discontent away from themselves, elites contribute to the antagonism by blaming economic downturns and other social catastrophes on middleman group intrigues. These accusations can result in mass killings, such as the infamous pogroms against Russian Jews.

The classic model has been criticized on several grounds. Some scholars assert that the classic middleman group model focuses exclusively on the historical experiences of permanent diasporas such as Jews and Armenians and consequently does not capture the experiences of contemporary ethnic groups that specialize in ethnic economies. Many modern societies do not disdain trade, and ethnic groups that concentrate in business do not possess a sojourning orientation or receive special favors from the elite. Other critics argue that the classic model places undue emphasis on class conflict and erroneously assumes that middleman groups passively accept stereotypes that others hold about them. An additional assumption of the classic model that does not apply in many contemporary societies is that middleman groups are socially impermeable and that their relations with the receiving society are purely economic.

As stated earlier, many of the critics of the classic model forget that it is an ideal type. Ideal types are analytic tools that represent abstractions from social or historical data. The fact that ideal types do not apply completely in many settings is not a shortcoming. Ideal types are devised precisely to analyze such departures from the abstracted features. We find the classic model useful as an ideal type because it identifies important variables in the study of middleman groups: duration of the middleman role, minority status of the group, use of precapitalist business practices, and relations between middleman groups and elites.

Duration of the middleman role depends on factors such as the existence of a fatherland to which the group may return, the availability of opportunities in the receiving society's general economy, and the group's capacity to take advantage of those opportunities. The transformation of the middleman group into a minority depends on such variables as the receiving society's tolerance, cultural differences between the group and the receiving society, and the existence of nationalist movements. Dependence on coethnic labor is associated with the supply of working-class coethnics and the abundance of working-class hosts. When the middleman group is not distinguished from the receiving society by cultural, linguistic, or religious differences, it tends to merge with the members of the receiving society, particularly the upper classes.

Cubans in Puerto Rico as a Middleman Group

Cubans in Puerto Rico have a socioeconomic profile that is typical of middleman groups in many respects. On the average, Cubans surpass Puerto Ricans in income, educational, and occupational levels. Cubans also show higher proportions of self-employed individuals and sales workers. Cubans who are not self-employed tend to work in businesses owned by coethnics or other outsiders.

Middleman businesses depend on the in-group for access to resources, dominate some business lines, serve an out-group clientele, and are dispersed throughout the host society. Cuban businesses in Puerto Rico conform to this pattern. First, Cuban entrepreneurs hire coethnics to occupy positions of trust in their businesses and rely on coethnics to form business partnerships. Second, Cuban firms concentrate in certain business lines, such as clothing stores, eating establishments, and mass media. Third, Cuban businesses depend principally on a Puerto Rican clientele and are spatially dispersed throughout San Juan and other cities.

Middleman group members are attached to the in-group, and this characteristic is found in the Cuban exile community. Cobas's survey showed that Cubans in Puerto Rico have a high proportion of friendships within the Cuban community. Duany's fieldwork found that Cubans tend to keep ritual kinship (*compadrazgo*) ties within the group and showed how Cubans struggle to preserve their cultural traditions and promote the group's prestige through organizations such as Casa Cuba and the Unión de Cubanos en el Exilio. The ethnic press has also supported in-group solidarity and identity.

As is the case for other middleman groups, Cubans have aroused host society antagonism. This hostility has three interrelated sources that are interrelated. First, popular stereotypes portray Cubans as jingoistic, boastful, loud, and self-important. Second, Cubans are perceived as opportunistic businessmen and unfair competitors who displace Puerto Ricans. Third, Cubans are seen as unconditional supporters of the United States and the cause of statehood for Puerto Rico.

Special circumstances influence the experiences of Cubans in Puerto Rico and cause them not to resemble the classic middleman group. First, despite some animosity toward Cubans in Puerto Rico, the degree of antagonism is moderate. Second, significant ties have developed between Cubans and their hosts. Those ties are best exemplified in a high exogamy rate among Cubans. It is important to remember, however, that the Puerto Rican partners in these exogamous marriages usually belong to the upper strata. The significant degree of exogamy and the moderate degree of host antagonism, though not typical, have historical precedents among other middleman groups whose culture, language, and religion are similar to those of the receiving societies. In such circumstances, the middleman group tends not to isolate itself.

Some students of middleman groups, such as Simmel and Bonacich and Modell, assert that clannishness and estrangement from the receiving society manifested by middleman groups have a utilitarian basis. In being clannish, individuals demonstrate their loyalty to the in-group and are in a better position to gain access to jobs or business resources. Estrangement supposedly originates in the businessmen's need to avoid close links with their customers, most of whom are out-group members.

Since cultural differences between Cubans and Puerto Ricans are minimal, it is possible to test this interpretation, and our results provide little support: neither employees in Cuban business nor business owners are more clannish than other group members. Age proved to be a better predictor of in-group attachment. This suggests that clannishness is more reflective of the patriotism of individuals who lived in Cuba longer than of the interests of ethnic economy members. To a great extent the absence of an exclusivist ideology among Cubans in Puerto Rico reflects self-protection. Ethnic economy members try to protect their reputation in the receiving society by minimizing their attachment to the in-group.

Regarding the estrangement hypothesis, ethnic business employees, but not the self-employed, show a greater sense of estrangement than do other group members. Employees have fewer economic investments and resources to protect themselves against outside attacks than owners. This is an important finding, because the literature presents ethnic business owners, not their employees, as the segment of the ethnic group that is most estranged from the receiving society.

Conclusion

Cubans in Puerto Rico have adapted as a middleman group. Their case shows, as did the experiences of Germans in Imperial Russia and Quakers and Scots in the United States and elsewhere, that a middleman group can spring up in situations in which the group is culturally similar to the receiving society. Moreover, this lack of cultural differences has mitigated the negative consequences that usually accompany the middleman position. Cubans have experienced only mild discrimination in Puerto Rico; members of the Puerto Rican upper classes, Catholics and Spanish-speakers like Cubans, have accepted them; Cubans and Puerto Ricans have intermarried—these developments, along with the lack of significant clannishness and estrangement among Cubans, suggest that Cubans will soon integrate with Puerto Rican society. As older Cubans die or out-migrate, their ethnic associations are likely to disappear. Unless a renewed influx of Cuban exiles occurs, Cubans will not remain in the middleman role permanently. Soon, Cubans will cease being the "Jews of the Caribbean."

Notes

Introduction

1. Sociologists employ the term *minority* usually to refer to a group that suffers from discrimination and prejudice from the receiving society. Not all middleman groups become minorities in this sense.

2. For this stage, the services of an expert in sampling, Dr. Miguel Valencia, were secured.

Chapter 1: Middleman Groups

1. Figure 1 does not represent a causal model but rather a diagram that helps summarize Bonacich's ideas on middleman groups.

2. Armstrong (1976, 394) refers to these groups as "archetypal mobilized diasporas."

3. For further discussion on similarities and differences between middleman groups and ethnic enclaves see Cobas (1987) and Waldinger et al. (1990).

Chapter 2: Background of the Cuban Exodus

1. Although Cuban migration to the United States and Puerto Rico can be traced to the middle of the nineteenth century, most scholarly studies have concentrated on migration after 1959. On Cubans in Tampa and Key West before 1898, see Pérez (1978), Middleton (1981), Poyo (1991), and Greenbaum (1985). On emigration following the 1959 Revolution, see in particular García (1996), Masud-Piloto (1996), Portes and Stepick (1993),

Pérez (1986), Portes and Bach (1985), Pedraza-Bailey (1985), Boswell and Curtis (1984), Casal and Hernández (1975), Rogg (1974), and Fagen et al. (1968). Recent studies on Cubans in Puerto Rico include Esteve (1984), Cobas (1985, 1986a, 1986b), Duany (1985b, 1987, 1989a, 1989b), Delgado Imbert (1989). For a review of Himilce Esteve's pioneering study, see Duany (1985a). Thus far, there are few studies on Cubans in Spain, Venezuela, and Mexico. A study on Cubans in Madrid appeared recently (Romano 1989).

2. For examples of triumphal articles on Cuban exiles see "Old Havana is Reborn in Miami," *Life,* September 12, 1966; "Those Amazing Cuban Emigrés," *Fortune,* October 1966; and "A Cuban Sucess Story in the United States," *U.S. News and World Report,* March 20, 1967. On the Mariel exodus, see the extensive list of articles in the popular press collected by Boswell and Rivero (1988). In a more rigorous tone, two researchers residing in Cuba assert that "45.25 percent of all individuals who left Cuba through the port of Mariel had delinquent backgrounds" (Hernández and Gomis 1986, 139).

3. For an analysis of U.S. policy toward the Mariel boatlift see Rivera (1982). According to Felix Masud-Piloto (1996), the U.S. government did not develop a coherent policy toward Cuban migration until the 1970s. In fact, the U.S. government has utilized Cuban immigration as part of a strategy to destabilize Castro's rule.

4. The Cuban government follows this practice in its own analysis of Cuban migration to the United States (Cuba, Comité Estatal de Estadísticas 1982, 60–79). For a sample of studies on Cuban migration conducted in Cuba, see Hernández (1985), Hernández and Gomis (1986), Valdés Paz (1983, 1987), and Rodríguez Chávez (1992).

5. Migration figures originating in Cuba do not always agree with those provided by American sources. Differences in data provided by Cuba's Comité Estatal de Estadísticas and Miami's Cuban Refugee Program are probably due to the arrival of Cuban immigrants through third countries and through clandestine means (compare Hernández 1985, 77; Jorge et al. 1991, 181).

6. From 1960 to 1970 about two hundred thousand Cuban exiles arrived in Spain. Most of them utilized Spain as a bridge to enter the United States (Romano 1989, 17).

7. A pamphlet issued by the Immigration and Naturalization Service defines a refugee as follows: "You are a refugee if you are unable or unwilling to return to your country because of persecution or a well-founded fear of persecution on account of race, religion, nationality, membership in a par-

ticular group, or political opinion." In practice, most refugees who came to the United States after World War II came from communist countries.

8. From January 1961 to December 1972 the Cuban Refugee Program helped relocate 296,806 exiles outside Miami (Masud-Piloto 1996, 53). By the end of 1971 the program had helped relocate 22,340 exiles to Puerto Rico (Prohías and Casal 1974, 18).

9. For an updated account of ethnic relations in Miami, see Portes and Stepick (1993).

10. For more details on the social origins of the Cuban ethnic enclave in Miami, see Portes (1987).

11. By 1980 about 63 percent of all Cubans in Puerto Rico were naturalized U.S. citizens (Esteve 1984, 26).

12. For additional recent data on the political, economic, and cultural importance of Cubans in Miami, see Jorge et al. (1991) and García (1996). For a discussion on the ideology of Cuban exiles in the United States, see Fernández (1987) and Torres (1988).

Chapter 3: Cuban Migration to Puerto Rico

1. Estimates of Puerto Rico's Cuban population range from 20,000 to 50,000 (Argüelles and McEoin 1982). The 1990 census counted 19,736 Cuban-born persons in Puerto Rico in addition to 2,882 persons with both Cuban parents, for a total of 22,618 persons of Cuban origin. Furthermore, 6,712 persons born in Puerto Rico had one Cuban parent (U.S. Department of Commerce 1993, tables 4 and 6).

2. On March 18, 1966, the following classified advertisements appeared in *El Mundo:* "Marlboro seeks Cubans for sales positions throughout the island" and "Cuban teacher will work with mentally retarded and slow-learning children." We are grateful to Himilce Esteve for making copies of these advertisements available to us.

3. In October 1990 the island's House of Representatives approved a similar resolution to study the impact of foreign population in Puerto Rico, but in this instance the catalyst was undocumented Dominican immigration. According to House Resolution 1770, "As the number of undocumented immigrants rises, so does the incidence of social problems, which results in a decrease in the quality of life in the communities in which these immigrants concentrate." On Dominican migration to Puerto Rico, see Duany (1990).

4. However, the most recent data from the Commonwealth's Elections Commission show that about thirty thousand individuals born outside Puerto Rico vote in local elections, including Cubans, Dominicans, and other foreign immigrants (*Claridad,* January 31–February 6, 1992).

5. On the exiles' expectations concerning a democratic change in Cuba, see the special report in the *San Juan Star,* November 3, 1991.

Chapter 4: Cubans in Puerto Rico as a Middleman Group

1. The discrepancy between the census data and Cobas's survey is probably due to the fact that Cobas's sample, limited to men, overrepresents self-employed Cuban workers in San Juan.

2. The substantial degree of Cuban exogamy is not due to an unbalance of the group's sex distribution, as happens in other settings. In 1980 the Cuban population of Puerto Rico had 92.8 men for every 100 women (U.S. Department of Commerce 1984b, table 95b). Further, the Cuban population does not show a preponderance of either sex in the prime marriage age, twenty to twenty-nine years old.

3. These data must be interpreted with caution. The sample is modest in size and does not represent all of the Cuban population of Puerto Rico.

Chapter 5: Consequences of Participation in the Ethnic Economy

1. This does not mean that Cubans and Puerto Ricans have not developed different symbols of ethnic identity. As we will show later, although cultural differences between the two groups are minimal, they can be played up.

2. Three levels of measurement are represented in the six dependent variables. One variable, Cuban friends, is continuous. Three dependent variables (Cuban partner, Cuban spouse, and Stranger) are ordinal, and the remaining two (Organizations and Citizen) are dichotomous. The appropriate technique for the continuous dependent variable is ordinary least squares regression. The correct method for the dichotomous dependent variables is binary logistic regression, and the appropriate technique for the ordinal dependent variables is a form of multinomial logistic regression called "proportional odds." For discussions of these statistical techniques see Agresti (1990); Hosmer and Lemeshow (1989); and Neter et al. (1969). Models were fitted using the SAS computer package. We employ the standard .05 level of significance in the statistical tests.

3. While ordinary least squares and binary logistic models produce one equation for each dependent variable, multinomial logistic models yield a number of equations equal to the number of categories in the dependent variable minus 1. For example, the multinomial logistic regression for the dependent variable Cuban Partner produces three different equations. In order to present results as clearly as possible, the coefficient estimates and corresponding standard errors are shown only for continuous and binary dependent variables. For multinomial models we present only the chi-square statistic and probability value associated with each independent variable. Finally, it is important to note that the SAS computer program prints results to several decimal places, and we found it necessary to round off for reasons of space. As a result of rounding off, there are minor discrepancies in the values of the t and chi-square statistics.

Chapter 6: La Casa Cuba

1. Virginia Domínguez, who conducted fieldwork among Cubans in New York, wrote that "There are no Cuban organizations whose primary focus is to further the interests of Cubans residing in the United States" (1975, 49). The situation has changed since the 1970s, particularly in Puerto Rico.

2. On Spanish émigré clubs in Cuba, see Kenny (1961); on Cuban clubs in Tampa before the revolution, see Middleton (1981) and Greenbaum (1985).

3. In Duany's survey 21 percent of the respondents were born in Oriente province, 13 percent in Las Villas, and 7 percent in Matanzas, compared to 42 percent in Havana.

4. The name *Círculo Cubano* is as old as Cuban migration to the United States; it was used as early as 1902 by cigar makers in Tampa (Middleton 1981, 295). In the 1980s Madrid had a Casa de Cuba with about six hundred members (Romano 1989, 68).

5. This estimate seems somewhat exaggerated. In Cobas's and Duany's studies, 17 percent of respondents were members of Casa Cuba.

6. This is not the first time that Casa Cuba has been publicly attacked in Puerto Rico. In 1971 the Juventud Cubana Socialista (an exile group that supports the revolution) asserted: "Well-known cases such as 'Casa Cuba,' where the same exclusiveness and racism of Havana's social clubs are practiced, are particularly shameful. We publicly disassociate ourselves from those attitudes, as well as from the unscrupulous business practices which characterize Cuban exiles in Puerto Rico" (Grupo Areíto 1978, 176).

7. Neither the political parties themselves nor the Electoral Commission of Puerto Rico provide statistics concerning the number of Cuban exiles registered with the different parties. Repeated attempts to obtain these data have been fruitless. However, data presented in chapter 4 confirm that Cubans tend to favor the pro-statehood PNP (Partido Nuevo Progresista).

Chapter 7: Cuban Associations in Puerto Rico

1. The labor force participation of Cuban women in Puerto Rico is relatively low. In 1990 about 46 percent of Cuban women over the age of sixteen were in the labor force of Puerto Rico (Rivera-Batiz and Santiago 1996). On the other hand, Cuban women in the United States had the highest labor force participation (55 percent) among Hispanics in 1980 (Prieto 1987, 74). The differences between Cuban women in Puerto Rico and the United States suggest that the former tend to belong to a higher social class than the latter.

2. Because the vast majority of Cuban exiles are Roman Catholic, their principal association is with the Catholic Church.

3. As pointed out in chapter 2, one of the most divisive issues among Cuban exiles has been the dialogue with the Cuban government. During 1978 UCE members hotly debated their position toward travel to Cuba by Cubans living abroad.

4. Bonacich and Modell (1980, 16) state that middleman groups are "noteworthy for their ability to take care of their own and not depend on public charity."

5. In 1978 Cuban exiles inaugurated a national sanctuary to Our Lady of Charity in Washington, D.C. Thousands of Cubans have since made pilgrimages to the sanctuary. The sanctuary dedicated to the Lady of Charity, built before the revolution in El Cobre, Cuba, continues to attract hundreds of believers.

6. Every year Cubans in Florida organize a similar, although more massive, event in a Miami stadium. In 1991 the Círculo Cubano sponsored a prayer vigil for the liberation of Cuba as part of its celebration of the feast of Our Lady of Charity.

7. As pointed out in chapter 1, Jews constitute a classic example of a "mobilized diaspora," an ethnic group that lacks a territorial base but enjoys material and cultural advantages over other ethnic groups, such as language and business skills (Armstrong 1976). In this regard Cuban exiles resemble the Jews.

8. This section on Cuban santería in Puerto Rico draws on several conversations with Cuban anthropologist Julio Sánchez, who has studied the phenomenon extensively.

9. A study at the end of the 1970s found that one of every four Cubans in the United States would resort to santería to obtain medical treatment if necessary (Díaz 1980, 13).

10. A 1991 survey ascertained that 36 percent of Cubans in Dade County favored some sort of dialogue with Castro's government. Seventy-three percent supported negotiations to facilitate travel of relatives in Cuba to the United States (Grenier and Gladwin 1991, 29, 43).

11. For more details about the socioeconomic background of Antonio Maceo Brigade members, see appendix 1, Grupo Areíto (1978, 137–43).

12. For more information about these groups, see Argüelles (1982, 37–38), Boswell and Curtis (1984, 171), and Torres (1988).

13. Among the associations not discussed here are Cuban Exiles' Rotary and Lion clubs; professional associations of architects, physicians, and educators; the Cuban Masonic Alliance; the Association of Alumni of Cuban Catholic Schools; and political organizations such as the Movimiento Demócrata Cristiano, Plataforma Democrática Cubana, and Cuba Independiente y Democrática, which will be discussed in chapter 8. In the early 1980s about thirty-five Cuban associations were active in Puerto Rico (Esteve 1984, 73).

14. In the 1990s Cuban associations in Puerto Rico have become politicized again as a result of changes in the relations among Cuba, the former Soviet Union, and Eastern Europe. However, the political ideology of the exiles is far from uniform, as is evident in the diversity of political responses to the economic crisis in Cuba.

Chapter 8: The Cuban Press in Puerto Rico

1. In the early 1980s Miami Spanish-language media included eight radio stations, two large newspapers, more than thirty weekly magazines, and a television station (Boswell and Curtis 1984, 119).

2. In addition, many Cuban exiles in Puerto Rico read *Diario Las Américas,* a newspaper published in Miami. For an analysis of *Diario Las Américas,* see Aguirre (1979).

3. In 1988 the second epoch of *Areíto* began; its editorial line is close to that of the original *Areíto.*

4. This is a common practice among Cuban tabloids in Miami, such as

Patria, Girón, and *Regreso.* See Argüelles (1982, 38–39) and Jorge et al. (1991, 91) for discussions of these publications.

5. Nonetheless, three members of exile organizations publicly refused the use of violence in their struggle against Fidel Castro. "We will not use terrorism as a means to combat Communist infiltration," declared Dr. Carlos Piñeiro, president of the Cuban Masonic Alliance, in a television interview held September 4, 1984. The other two exiles were Orlando Canales and Julio Labatut. In addition, Cuban exile organizations such as UCE have condemned terrorism as a "criminal and anti-Christian fighting method" (*Unión,* 16, no. 85, 1977, 3).

6. *Vida de club* is a typical exile family business. Jorge Cunill is the editor, his wife Liliana is the executive coordinator, and their daughter Lilibí is in charge of youth matters.

7. Women in Spain and Latin America traditionally do not replace their own surnames with their husbands' upon marriage. However, they may add their husbands' names to their own. For example, María Rodríguez, who married José García, may choose to call herself María Rodríguez de García.

8. The author is a Cuban dentist who is well connected with exile organizations such as the Círculo Cubano, the UCE, the Cuban Rotary Club, 2506 Brigade, and the Medical Association in Exile.

9. We quote from several columns published in April and May 1984.

10. Argüelles suggests that Miami's Cuban press "reinforces the exiles' insecurity and paranoia, promotes their passive aggressiveness, and places them in the hands of avid *santeros*" (1982, 39). Puerto Rico's Cuban press plays a more limited role.

Bibliography

Agresti, Alan

1990 *Categorical Data Analysis.* New York: Wiley.

Aguirre, Benigno

1992 "Cuban Mass Migration and the Social Construction of Deviance." Paper presented at the 14th meeting of the Instituto de Estudios Cubanos, Rollins College, Winter Park, Florida, June 26–27.

1979 "Ethnic Newspapers and Politics: *Diario Las Américas* and the Watergate Affair." *Ethnic Groups* 2(2):155–65.

Aldrich, Howard, and Roger Waldinger

1990 "Ethnicity and Entrepreneurship." *Annual Review of Sociology* 16:111–35.

Amaro, Nelson, and Carmelo Mesa-Lago

1971 "Inequality and Classes." In *Revolutionary Change in Cuba,* edited by Carmelo Mesa-Lago, 341–74. Pittsburgh: University of Pittsburgh Press.

Amaro, Nelson, and Alejandro Portes

1972 "Notas para una sociología del exilio: Situación y perspectivas de los grupos cubanos en EEUU." *Aportes* 23:7–24.

Arana-Soto, S.

1963 *Cuba y Puerto Rico no son . . . o la enfermedad de Cuba.* San Juan: Luis D. Paret.

Argüelles, Lourdes

1982 "Cuban Miami: The Roots, Development, and Everyday Life of an Emigré Enclave in the U.S. National Security State." *Contemporary Marxism* 5:27–43.

Argüelles, Lourdes, and Gary McEoin

1982 "Cubanos emigrados en P.R.: Coloniaje y terrorismo." *Areíto* 8(31):41–46.

Armstrong, John A.
1976 "Mobilized and Proletarian Diasporas." *American Political Science Review* 70(2):393–408.

Azicri, Max
1982 "The Politics of Exile: Trends and Dynamics of Political Change Among Cuban-Americans." *Cuban Studies/Estudios cubanos* 11(2):54–73.

Bach, Robert L.
1988 *Migration as an Issue in U.S.-Cuban Relations*. Occasional Paper No. 20, Central American and Caribbean Program, School of Advanced International Studies, Johns Hopkins University.
1982 "The New Cuban Exodus: Political and Economic Motivations." *Caribbean Review* 11(2):22–25, 58–60.

Becker, Howard P.
1956 *Man in Reciprocity: Introductory Lectures on Culture, Society, and Personality*. New York: Praeger.

Blalock, Hubert
1967 *Toward a Theory of Minority Group Relations*. New York: Wiley.

Bonacich, Edna
1987 "Making It in America: A Social Evaluation of the Ethics of Immigrant Entrepreneurship." *Sociological Perspectives* 30:446–66.
1973 "A Theory of Middleman Minorities." *American Sociological Review* 38(5):583–94.

Bonacich, Edna, Ivan Light, and Charles Choy Wong
1980 "Korean Immigrant Small Business in Los Angeles." In *Sourcebook on the New Immigration: Implications for the United States and the International Community*, edited by Roy Simón Bryce-Laporte, Delores Mortimer, and Stephen R. Couch, 167–84. New Brunswick, N.J.: Trans-Action Books.

Bonacich, Edna, and John Modell
1980 *The Economic Basis of Ethnic Solidarity: Small Business in the Japanese American Community*. Berkeley: University of California Press.

Borrás, Gloria
1984 "Cuba: El exilio en Puerto Rico." *El Mundo* (San Juan), January 1.

Boswell, Thomas D., and James R. Curtis
1984 *The Cuban-American Experience: Culture, Images, and Perspectives*. Totowa, N.J.: Rowman and Allanheld.

Boswell, Thomas D., and Manuel Rivero
1988 *Bibliography for the Mariel-Cuban Diaspora.* Occasional Paper no. 7, Center for Latin American Studies, University of Florida, Gainesville.

Brigada Antonio Maceo
1983a "Puntos de unidad del V Contingente." Unpublished manuscript in possession of the authors.
1983b "Reglamento del V Contingente." Unpublished manuscript in possession of the authors.

Butterworth, Douglas S., and John K. Chance
1981 *Latin American Urbanization.* Cambridge: Cambridge University Press.

Cahman, Walter P.
1957 "Socioeconomic Causes of Antisemitism." *Social Problems* 5:21–29.

Carr, Raymond
1984 *Puerto Rico: A Colonial Experiment.* New York: New York University Press.

Casal, Lourdes
1979 "Cubans in the United States: Their Impact on U.S.-Cuban Relations." In *Revolutionary Cuba in the World Arena,* edited by Martin Weinstein, 109–35. Philadelphia: Institute for the Study of Human Issues.

Casal, Lourdes, and Andrés Hernández
1975 "Cubans in the U.S.: A Review of the Literature." *Cuban Studies/Estudios cubanos* 5(2):25–51.

Castile, George Pierre, and Gilbert Kushner, eds.
1981 *Persistent Peoples: Cultural Enclaves in Perspective.* Tucson: University of Arizona Press.

Cherry, Robert
1989 "Middleman Minority Theories: Their Implications for Black-Jewish Relations." *Journal of Ethnic Studies* 17(4):117–38.

Círculo Cubano de Puerto Rico
1980 *Círculo Cubano de Puerto Rico, 1949–1980: Historia de la Casa Cuba.* San Juan: Círculo Cubano de Puerto Rico.
1979 *Reglamento.* Isla Verde, P.R.

Clark, Juan M.
1990 *Cuba: Mito y realidad. Testimonios de un pueblo.* Caracas: Saeta.
1983 "El éxodo cubano, 1959–1980." In *UCE/20 años,* edited by Unión de Cubanos en el Exilio, 39–46. San Juan.

Clark, Juan M., José I. Lasaga, and Rose S. Reque

1981 *The 1980 Mariel Exodus: An Assessment and Prospect.* Washington, D.C.: Council for Interamerican Security.

Cobas, José A.

1987 "Ethnic Enclaves and Middleman Minorities: Alternative Strategies of Immigrant Adaptation?" *Sociological Perspectives* 30(2):143–61.

1986a "Paths to Self-Employment Among Immigrants: An Analysis of Four Interpretations." *Sociological Perspectives* 29(1):101–20.

1986b "Puerto Rican Reactions to Cuban Immigrants: Insights from Trading Minority Interpretations." *Ethnic and Racial Studies* 9(4):529–36.

1985 "A New Test and Extension of Propositions from the Bonacich Synthesis." *Social Forces* 64(2):432–41.

Cohen, Abner

1969 *Custom and Politics in Urban Africa: A Study of Hausa Migrants in Yoruba Towns.* Berkeley: University of California Press.

Cooney, Rosemary Santana, and María Alina Contreras

1978 "Residence Patterns of Social Register Cubans: A Study of Miami, San Juan and New York SMSAs." *Cuban Studies/Estudios cubanos* 8(2):33–49.

Cuba, Comité Estatal de Estadísticas

1982 *Estadísticas de migraciones externas y turismo.* Havana: Editorial Orbe.

Cué, Reynaldo, and Robert L. Bach

1980 "The Return of the Clandestine Worker and the End of the Golden Exile: Recent Mexican and Cuban Immigrants in the United States." In *Sourcebook on the New Immigration: Implications for the United States and the International Community,* edited by Roy Simón Bryce-Laporte, Delores Mortimer, and Stephen R. Couch, 257–69. New Brunswick, N.J.: Trans-Action Books.

Delgado Imbert, María del Pilar

1989 "El exilio cubano en Puerto Rico: Su aportación cultural." Ph.D. diss., University of Valladolid.

Díaz, Guarioné, ed.

1980 *Evaluation and Identification of Policy Issues in the Cuban Community.* Miami: Cuban National Planning Council.

Díaz-Briquets, Sergio

1984 "Cuban-Owned Businesses in the United States." *Cuban Studies/Estudios cubanos* 14(2):57–64.

Domínguez, Virginia R.

1975 *From Neighbor to Stranger: The Dilemma of Caribbean Peoples in the United States.* Occasional Paper no. 5, Antilles Research Program, Yale University.

1973 "Spanish-Speaking Caribbeans in New York: 'The Middle Race.'" *Revista/Review Interamericana* 3(2):135–42.

Duany, Jorge

1992 "Caribbean Migration to Puerto Rico: A Comparison of Cubans and Dominicans." *International Migration Review* 26(1):46–66.

1989a "Ethnic Identity and Socioeconomic Adaptation: The Case of Cubans in Puerto Rico." *Journal of Ethnic Studies* 17(1):109–27.

1989b "The Cuban Community in Puerto Rico: A Comparative Caribbean Perspective." *Ethnic and Racial Studies* 12(1):36–46.

1987 "Buscando ambiente: Estratificación social y minorías étnicas en San Juan, Puerto Rico." *Revista de ciencias sociales* 26(1):103–38.

1985a Review of *Himilce Esteve, El exilio cubano en Puerto Rico: Su impacto político-social, 1959–1983. Cuban Studies/Estudios cubanos* 15(1):75–78.

1985b "The Cubans of Puerto Rico: Socioeconomic Adaptation in a Caribbean City." Ph.D. diss., University of California, Berkeley.

1982 "Stones, Trees, and Blood: An Analysis of a Cuban Santero Ritual." *Cuban Studies/Estudios cubanos* 12(2):37–53.

1979 "The New Man in Cuba: Social Attitude Change After the Revolution." Master's thesis, University of Chicago.

Duany, Jorge, ed.

1990 *Los dominicanos en Puerto Rico: Migración en la semi-periferia.* Río Piedras, P.R.: Huracán.

Eller, Jack D., and Reed M. Coughlan

1990 "The Poverty of Primordialism: The Demystification of Ethnic Attachments." *Ethnic and Racial Studies* 16:183–202.

Esteve, Himilce

1984 *El exilio cubano en Puerto Rico: Su impacto político-social, 1959–1983.* San Juan: Raíces.

Fagen, Richard R., Richard A. Brody, and Thomas J. O'Leary

1968 *Cubans in Exile: Disaffection and the Revolution.* Stanford: Stanford University Press.

Fernández, Damián J.

1987 "From Little Havana to Washington, D.C.: The Impact of Cuban-Americans on U.S. Foreign Policy." In *Ethnic Groups and Foreign Policy,* edited by Mohammed Ahrari. Westport, Conn.: Greenwood Press.

Fitzpatrick, Joseph P., and Douglas T. Gurak
1979 *Hispanic Intermarriage in New York City: 1975.* New York: Hispanic Research Center, Fordham University.

Foster, Brian L.
1974 "Ethnicity and Commerce." *American Ethnologist* 1(3):437–48.

Freire, Joaquín
1966 *Presencia de Puerto Rico en la historia de Cuba (una aportación al estudio de la historia antillana).* San Juan: Instituto de Cultura Puertorriqueña.

Fried, Morton
1958 "The Chinese in British Guiana." In *Colloquium on Overseas Chinese,* edited by Morton Fried. New York: Institute of Pacific Relations.

García, María Cristina
1996 *Havana USA: Cuban Exiles and Cuban Americans in South Florida, 1959–1994.* Berkeley: University of California Press.

Garrison, Bruce
1987 "The Upscale Hispanic Magazine Reader: Acculturation and the 'Yucca' Lifestyle." Paper presented at the 70th annual meeting of the Association for Education in Journalism and Mass Communication, San Antonio, Texas, August 14. (ERIC Document 283 157.)

Geertz, Clifford
1963 *Peddlers and Princes: Social Change and Economic Modernization in Two Indonesian Towns.* Chicago: University of Chicago Press.

González, Antonio J.
1970 "Estudio sobre el impacto de la inmigración en Puerto Rico." *Revista del Colegio de Abogados de Puerto Rico* 31(4):619–47.

González, José Luis
1986 *Nueva visita al cuarto piso.* Madrid: Colección del Flamboyán.

Greenbaum, Susan D.
1985 "Afro-Cubans in Exile: Tampa, Florida, 1886–1984." *Cuban Studies/Estudios cubanos* 15(1):59–72.

Grenier, Guillermo J.
1990 "Ethnic Solidarity and the Cuban-American Labor Movement in Dade County." *Cuban Studies* 20:29–48.

Grenier, Guillermo J., and Hugh Gladwin

1991 *Views on Policy Options toward Cuba Held by Cuban-American Residents of Dade County, Florida.* Miami: Institute of Public Opinion Research, Florida International University.

Grupo Areíto

1978 *Contra viento y marea: Jóvenes cubanos hablan desde su exilio en Estados Unidos.* Ciudad de México: Siglo Veintiuno.

Hahner, June E.

1976 "Jacobinos versus Galegos: Urban Radicals versus Portuguese Immigrants in Rio de Janeiro in the 1890s." *Journal of Interamerican Studies and World Affairs* 18:125–54.

Hermandad de la Caridad

1983 *Anuario de la Caridad.* San Juan: Ramallo.

Hernández, Andrés, ed.

1974 *The Cuban Minority in the U.S.: Final Report and Need Identification.* Washington, D.C.: Cuban National Planning Council.

Hernández, Rafael

1985 "La política de los Estados Unidos hacia Cuba y la cuestión de la migración." *Cuadernos de Nuestra América* 2(3):75–100.

Hernández, Rafael, and Hugo Azcuy

1990 "Relaciones Cuba-USA: La libertad de migrar." *Bohemia* 82(35):46–49.

Hernández, Rafael, and Redi Gomis

1986 "Retrato del Mariel: El ángulo socioeconómico." *Cuadernos de Nuestra América* 3(5):124–51.

Horowitz, Donald L.

1985 *Ethnic Groups in Conflict.* Berkeley: University of California Press.

Hosmer, David W., and Stanley Lemeshow

1989 *Applied Logistic Regression.* New York: Wiley.

Jorge, Antonio, Jaime Suchlicki, and Adolfo Leyva de Varona, eds.

1991 *Cuban Exiles in Florida: Their Presence and Contribution.* Miami: Research Institute for Cuban Studies, University of Miami.

Kenny, Michael

1961 "Twentieth Century Spanish Expatriates in Cuba: A Sub-Culture?" *Anthropological Quarterly* 34(2):85–93.

Landon, Kenneth Perry

1941 *The Chinese in Thailand.* New York: Russell and Russell.

Leon, Abram

1970 *The Jewish Question: A Marxist Interpretation.* New York: Pathfinder.

Lewis, Gordon K.
1974 *Notes on the Puerto Rican Revolution: An Essay on American Dominance and Puerto Rican Resistance.* New York: Monthly Review Press.

Lewis, Oscar, et al.
1977–78 *Living the Revolution: An Oral History of Contemporary Cuba.* 3 vols. Urbana: University of Illinois Press.

Light, Ivan
1984 "Immigrant and Ethnic Enterprise in North America." *Ethnic and Racial Studies* 7(2):195–216.
1972 *Ethnic Enterprise in America: Business and Welfare Among Chinese, Japanese, and Blacks.* Berkeley: University of California Press.

Light, Ivan, and Edna Bonacich
1988 *Immigrant Entrepreneurs: Koreans in Los Angeles, 1965–1982.* Berkeley: University of California Press.

Light, Ivan, Georges Sabagh, Mehdi Bozorgmehr, and Claudia Der-Martirosian
1994 "Beyond the Ethnic Enclave Economy." *Social Problems* 41(1):65–80.

Mackey, William Francis, and Von Nieda Beebe
1977 *Bilingual Schools for a Bicultural Community: Miami's Adaptation to the Cuban Refugees.* Rowley, Mass.: Newbury House.

Maldonado, A. W.
1972 "El problema de los cubanos." *El Mundo,* November 26, p. 7A.

Maldonado Denis, Manuel
1972 *Puerto Rico: A Socio-Historic Interpretation.* New York: Random House.

Marqués, René
1977 *El puertorriqueño dócil y otros ensayos (1953–1971).* San Juan: Antillana.

Marx, Karl
1964 "On the Jewish Question." In *Early Writings,* 1–40. New York: McGraw-Hill.

Masud-Piloto, Félix
1996 *From Welcomed Exiles to Illegal Immigrants: Cuban Migration to the U.S., 1959–1995.* Lanham, Md.: Rowman and Littlefield.

McGaffey, Wyatt, and Clifford R. Barnett
1962 *Cuba: Its People, Its Society, Its Culture.* New Haven: HRAF Press.

Middleton, DeWight R.
1981 "The Organization of Ethnicity in Tampa." *Ethnic Groups* 3(4):281–305.

Montaner, Carlos Alberto
1971 *Impacto de la emigración cubana en el Puerto Rico actual.* Río Piedras, P.R.: Editorial San Juan.

Montero Seplowin, Virginia
1964 "The Cubans in Puerto Rico." *San Juan Review* 1(4):8–12.

Neter, John, Michael Wasserman, and Michael H. Kutner
1989 *Applied Linear Regression Models.* Homewood, Ill.: Irwin.

Park, Robert E.
1950a "Human Migration and the Marginal Man." In *Race and Culture,* 345–56. Glencoe: Free Press.
1950b "The Nature of Race Relations." In *Race and Culture,* 81–116. Glencoe: Free Press.

Patterson, Orlando
1975 "Context and Choice in Ethnic Allegiance: A Theoretical Framework and Caribbean Case Study." In *Ethnicity: Theory and Experience,* edited by Mathan Glazer and Daniel P. Moynihan, 305–49. Cambridge, Mass.: Harvard University Press.

Pedraza-Bailey, Silvia
1985 *Political and Economic Migrants in America: Cubans and Mexicans.* Austin: University of Texas Press.

Pérez, Lisandro
1986 "Cubans in the United States." *Annals of the American Academy of Political and Social Science* 487:126–37.
1980 "Cubans." In *Harvard Encyclopedia of American Ethnic Groups,* edited by Stephan Thernstrom et al. Cambridge, Mass.: Belknap Press.

Pérez, Louis J., Jr.
1978 "Cubans in Tampa: From Exiles to Immigrants, 1892–1901." *Florida Historical Quarterly* 53(2):129–40.

Pérez Cruz, Sylvia
1978 "Características demográficas, sociales y económicas de la población cubana residente en Puerto Rico, 1970." Master's thesis, University of Puerto Rico.

Pettigrew, Thomas F., George M. Frederickson, Dale T. Knobel, Nathan Glazer, and Reed Ueda
1982 *Prejudice.* Cambridge, Mass.: Harvard University Press.

Picó de Hernández, Isabel, Marcia Rivera, Carmen Parrilla, Jeannette Ramos de Sánchez Vilella, and Isabelo Zenón
1985 *Discrimen por color, sexo y origen nacional en Puerto Rico.* Río

Piedras, P.R.: Centro de Investigaciones Sociales, Universidad de Puerto Rico.

Portes, Alejandro

1987 "The Social Origins of the Cuban Enclave Economy of Miami." *Sociological Perspectives* 30(4):340–72.

1984 "The Rise of Ethnicity: Determinants of Ethnic Perceptions Among Cuban Exiles in Miami." *American Sociological Review* 49(3):383–97.

1969 "Dilemmas of a Golden Exile: Integration of Cuban Refugee Families in Milwaukee." *American Sociological Review* 34(4):505–18.

Portes, Alejandro, and Robert L. Bach

1985 *Latin Journey: Cuban and Mexican Immigrants in the United States.* Berkeley: University of California Press.

Portes, Alejandro, and Jozsef Borocz

1989 "Contemporary Immigration: Theoretical Perspectives on its Determinants and Modes of Incorporation." *International Migration Review* 23(3):606–30.

Portes, Alejandro, Juan M. Clark, and Robert L. Bach

1977 "The New Wave: A Statistical Profile of Recent Cuban Exiles to the United States." *Cuban Studies/Estudios Cubanos* 7(1):1–32.

Portes, Alejandro, Juan M. Clark, and Manuel López

1981–82 "Six Years Later, the Process of Incorporation of Cuban Exiles in the United States: 1973–1979." *Cuban Studies/Estudios cubanos* 11(2)/12(1):1–24.

Portes, Alejandro, and Robert D. Manning

1986 "The Immigrant Enclave: Theory and Empirical Examples." In *Competitive Ethnic Relations,* edited by Joane Nagel and Susan Olzak, 47–68. Orlando, Fla.: Academic Press.

Portes, Alejandro, and Rafael Mozo

1985 "The Political Adaptation of Cubans and Other Ethnic Minorities in the United States: A Preliminary Analysis." *International Migration Review* 19(1):35–65.

Portes, Alejandro, and Alex Stepick

1993 *City on the Edge: The Transformation of Miami.* Berkeley: University of California Press.

Posada, Joaquín de, ed.

1973–80 *Anuario de familias cubanas.* San Juan: Graficart.

Poyo, Gerald E.

1991 "The Cuban Experience in the United States, 1865–1940: Migration, Community, and Identity." *Cuban Studies* 21:19–36.

Prieto, Yolanda
1987 "Cuban Women in the U.S. Labor Force: Perspectives on the Nature of Change." *Cuban Studies* 17:73–91.
Prohías, Rafael J., and Lourdes Casal
1974 *The Cuban Minority in the U.S.: Preliminary Report on Need Identification and Program Evaluation.* Washington, D.C.: Cuban National Planning Council.
Publicidad Badillo
1967 "Estudio sobre la contribución económica de empresas y negocios cubanos en Puerto Rico." Unpublished manuscript in possession of the authors.
Purcell, Victor
1948 *The Chinese in Malaya.* London: Oxford University Press.
Rinder, Irin
1958 "Strangers in the Land: Social Relations in the Status Gap." *Social Problems* 6:253–60.
Rivera, Mario A.
1982 "An Evaluative Analysis of the Carter Administration's Policy Toward the Mariel Influx of 1980." Ph.D. diss., University of Notre Dame.
Rivera-Batiz, Francisco, and Carlos E. Santiago
1995 *Island Paradox: Puerto Rico in the 1990s.* New York: Russell Sage.
Rodríguez Chávez, Ernesto
1992 "El patrón migratorio cubano: Cambio y continuidad." *Cuadernos de Nuestra América* 9(18):77–95.
Rogg, Eleanor Meyer
1974 *The Assimilation of Cuban Exiles: The Role of Community and Class.* New York: Aberdeen.
Rogg, Eleanor Meyer, and Rosemary Santana Cooney
1980 *Adaptation and Adjustment of Cubans: West New York, New Jersey.* Monograph no. 5, Hispanic Research Center, Fordham University.
Romano, Vicente
1989 *Cuba en el corazón: Testimonios de un desarraigo.* Barcelona: Antropos.
Royce, Anya Peterson
1982 *Ethnic Identity: Strategies of Diversity.* Bloomington: Indiana University Press.
Rumbaut, Rubén G.
1984 "Experiencia del exilio: Crisis, compromiso e identidad." *Areíto* 9(36):37–39.

Safa, Elie
1960 *L'émigration libanaise.* Beirut: Université Saint-Joseph.
Safa, Helen Icken
1974 *The Urban Poor of Puerto Rico: A Study in Development and Inequality.* New York: Holt, Rinehart and Winston.
Sánchez, Julio
1978 *La religión de los orichas: Creencias y ceremonias de un culto afrocaribeño.* San Juan: Ramallo.
Sandoval, Mercedes C.
1979 "Santería as a Mental Health Care System: An Historical Overview." *Social Science and Medicine* 13b(2):137–51.
Scott, George M.
1990 "A Resynthesis of the Primordial and Circumstancial Approaches to Ethnic Group Solidarity: Towards an Explanatory Model." *Ethnic and Racial Studies* 13:147–71.
Shils, Edward
1975 *Center and Periphery: Essays in Macrosociology.* Vol. 2. Chicago: University of Chicago Press.
Simmel, Georg
1964 "The Stranger." In *The Sociology of Georg Simmel,* edited by Kurt H. Wolff, 402–8. New York: Free Press.
Skinner, G. William
1957 *Chinese Society in Thailand: An Analytical History.* Ithaca: Cornell University Press.
Stonequist, Everett V.
1937 *The Marginal Man: A Study in Personality and Culture Conflict.* New York: Russell and Russell.
Stryker, Sheldon
1958 "Social Structure and Prejudice." *Social Problems* 6:340–54.
Torres, María de los Angeles
1988 "From Exiles to Minorities: The Politics of Cuban-Americans." In *Latinos and the Political System,* edited by F. Chris García, 81–98. Notre Dame: University of Notre Dame Press.
Treiman, Donald J.
1977 *Occupational Prestige in Comparative Perspective.* New York: Academic Press.
Unión de Cubanos en el Exilio
1991 *UCE/1962–1991: Puerto Rico.* San Juan.

1986 "Reglamento UCE: Capítulo de San Juan de Puerto Rico." Unpublished manuscript in possession of the authors.
1984 *UCE/1962–1984: Puerto Rico.* San Juan.
1983 *UCE/20 años.* Hato Rey: Ramallo.

U.S. Department of Commerce, Bureau of the Census
1993 *1990 Census of Population: Social and Economic Characteristics. Puerto Rico.* Washington, D.C.: U.S. Government Printing Office.
1991 *The Hispanic Population in the United States: March 1990.* Washington, D.C.: U.S. Government Printing Office.
1984a *1980 Census of Population: General Social and Economic Characteristics, Puerto Rico.* Washington, D.C.: U.S. Government Printing Office.
1984b *1980 Census of Population and Housing: Detailed Population Characteristics, Puerto Rico.* Washington, D.C.: U.S. Government Printing Office.

U.S. Department of Justice
1992 *1992 Statistical Yearbook of Immigration and Naturalization Service.* Washington, D.C.: U.S. Government Printing Office.
1988 *1988 Statistical Yearbook of Immigration and Naturalization Service.* Washington, D.C.: U.S. Government Printing Office.
1980 "Foreigners Registered in Puerto Rico." Unpublished manuscript in possession of the authors.
1978 *Our Immigration: A Brief Account of Immigration to the United States.* Washington, D.C.: U.S. Government Printing Office.

Valdés Paz, Juan
1987 "La aculturación de la comunidad cubana en los Estados Unidos." *Cuadernos de Nuestra América* 4(7):160–218.
1983 "La estructura de clase de la comunidad cubana en los Estados Unidos." *Cuadernos de Nuestra América* 1:5–35.

Vázquez Calzada, José L., and Zoraida Morales del Valle
1979a "Características de la población extranjera residente en Puerto Rico." *Revista de ciencias sociales* 21(3–4):245–88.
1979b "Características socio-demográficas de los norteamericanos, cubanos y dominicanos residentes en Puerto Rico." *Revista de ciencias sociales* 21(1–2):1–34.

Volsky, George
1974 "Cubans in Puerto Rico Discover Both Warmth and Resentment." *New York Times,* February 3, p. 22.

Waldinger, Roger
1984 "Immigrant Enterprise in the New York Garment Industry." *Social Problems* 32:60–71.

Waldinger, Roger, Howard Aldrich, Robin Ward, and others
1990 *Ethnic Entrepreneurs: Immigrant Business in Industrial Societies.* Newbury Park, Calif.: Sage Publications.

Wallman, Sandra
1979 "Introduction." In *Ethnicity at Work,* edited by Sandra Wallman, i–xii. London: Macmillan.

Weber, Max
1978a *Economy and Society: An Outline of Interpretive Sociology.* Berkeley: University of California Press.
1978b "The Great Religions of the World." In *Economy and Society: An Outline of Interpretive Sociology,* 1:611–40. Berkeley: University of California Press.
1958 *The Protestant Ethic and the Spirit of Capitalism.* New York: Scribners.

Wilson, Kenneth, and W. Allen Martin
1982 "Ethnic Enclaves: A Comparison of the Cuban and Black Economies of Miami." *American Journal of Sociology* 88(1):135–60.

Wilson, Kenneth, and Alejandro Portes
1980 "Immigrant Enclaves: An Analysis of the Labor Market Experiences of Cubans in Miami." *American Journal of Sociology* 86(2):295–319.

Wong, Eugene F.
1985 "Asian American Middleman Minority Theory: The Framework of an American Myth." *Journal of Ethnic Studies* 13(1):51–88.

Zenner, Walter P.
1991 *Minorities in the Middle: A Cross-Cultural Analysis.* Albany: State University of New York Press.

Index